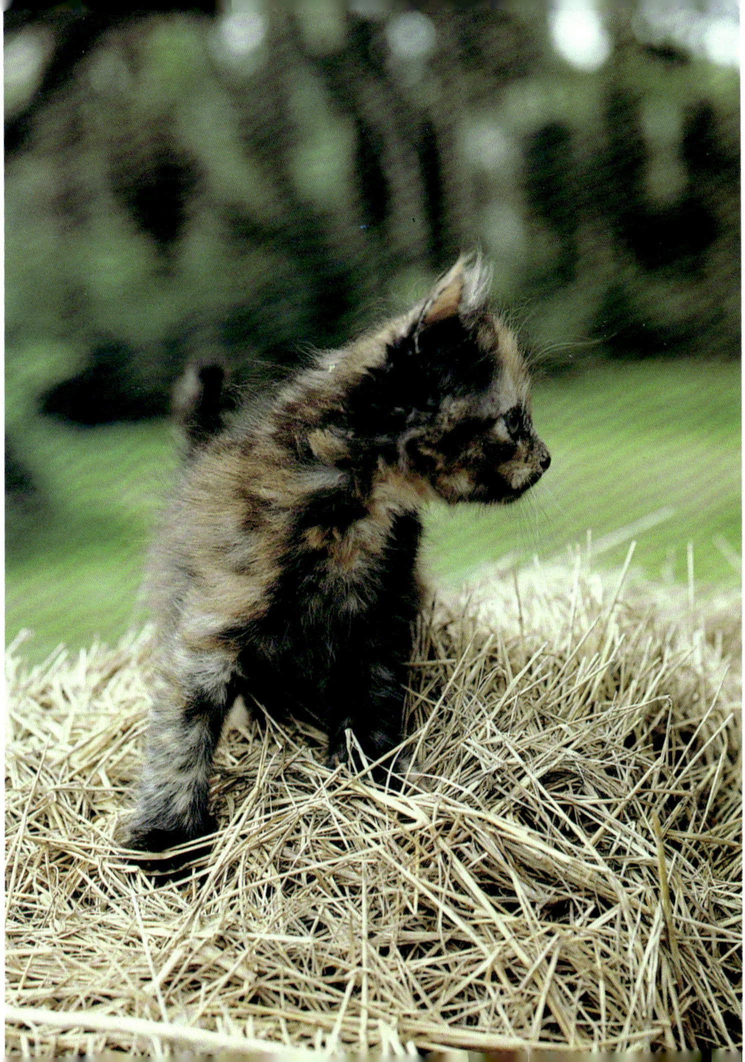

The Quotable
Barn Cat

Norvia Behling

Voyageur Press

First published in 2007 by Voyageur Press, an imprint of MBI Publishing Company, Galtier Plaza, Suite 200, 380 Jackson Street, St. Paul, MN 55101 USA

Copyright © 2007 by Norvia Behling

All rights reserved. With the exception of quoting brief passages for the purposes of review, no part of this publication may be reproduced without prior written permission from the Publisher.

The information in this book is true and complete to the best of our knowledge. All recommendations are made without any guarantee on the part of the author or Publisher, who also disclaim any liability incurred in connection with the use of this data or specific details.

We recognize, further, that some words, model names, and designations mentioned herein are the property of the trademark holder. We use them for identification purposes only. This is not an official publication.

Voyageur Press titles are also available at discounts in bulk quantity for industrial or sales-promotional use. For details write to Special Sales Manager at MBI Publishing Company, Galtier Plaza, Suite 200, 380 Jackson Street, St. Paul, MN 55101 USA.

To find out more about our books, join us online at www.VoyageurPress.com.

All photography by Norvia Behling except for on pages 12, 23, 38, and 95 by Daniel Johnson and on pages 5, 41, and 46 by Connie Summers.

Editor: Amy Glaser
Designer: Jennifer Bergstrom

Printed in China

Library of Congress Cataloging-in-Publication Data

The quotable barn cat / [compiled] by Norvia Behling.
  p. cm.
  "Editor: Amy Glaser."
  ISBN-13: 978-0-7603-2908-5 (hardbound w/ jacket)
  ISBN-10: 0-7603-2908-7 (hardbound w/ jacket) 1. Cats--Quotations, maxims, etc. I. Behling, Norvia. II. Glaser, Amy.
  PN6084.C23Q65 2007
  636.8--dc22

2007002667

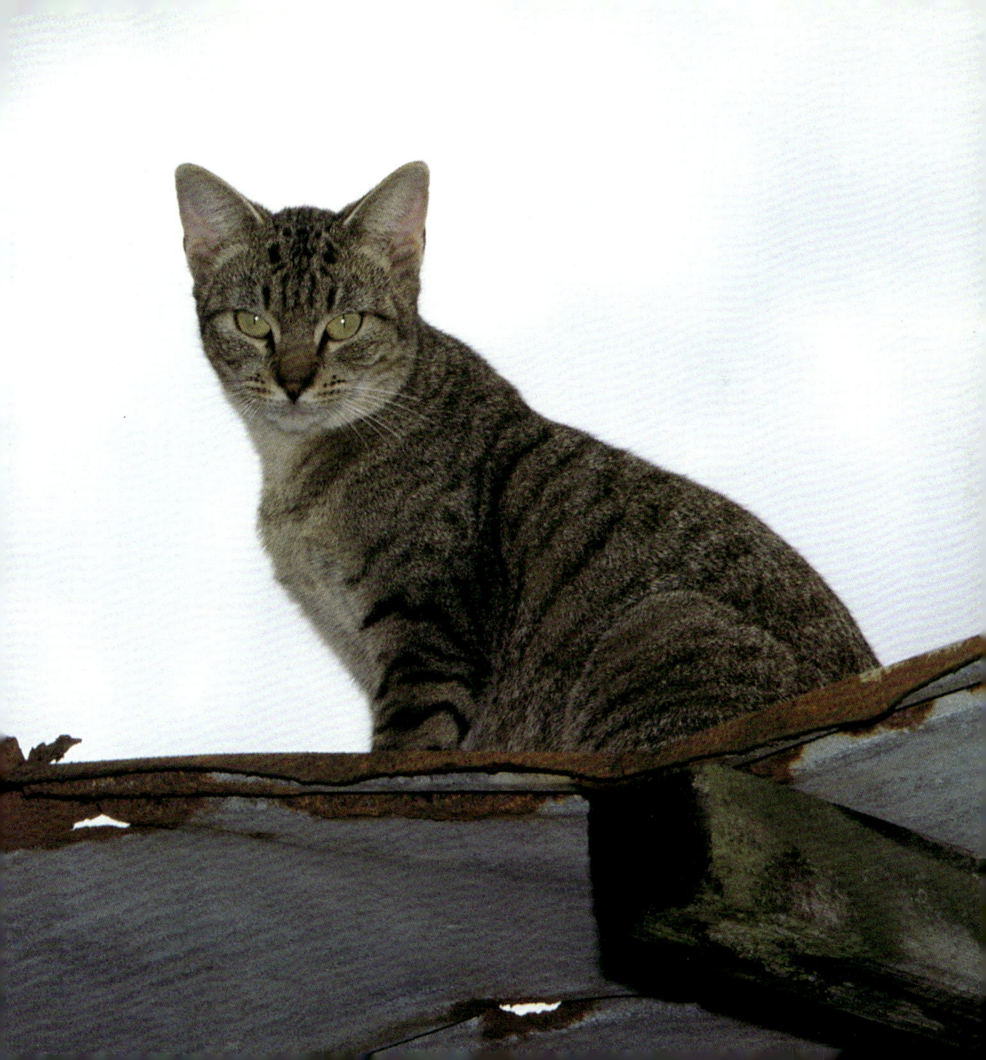

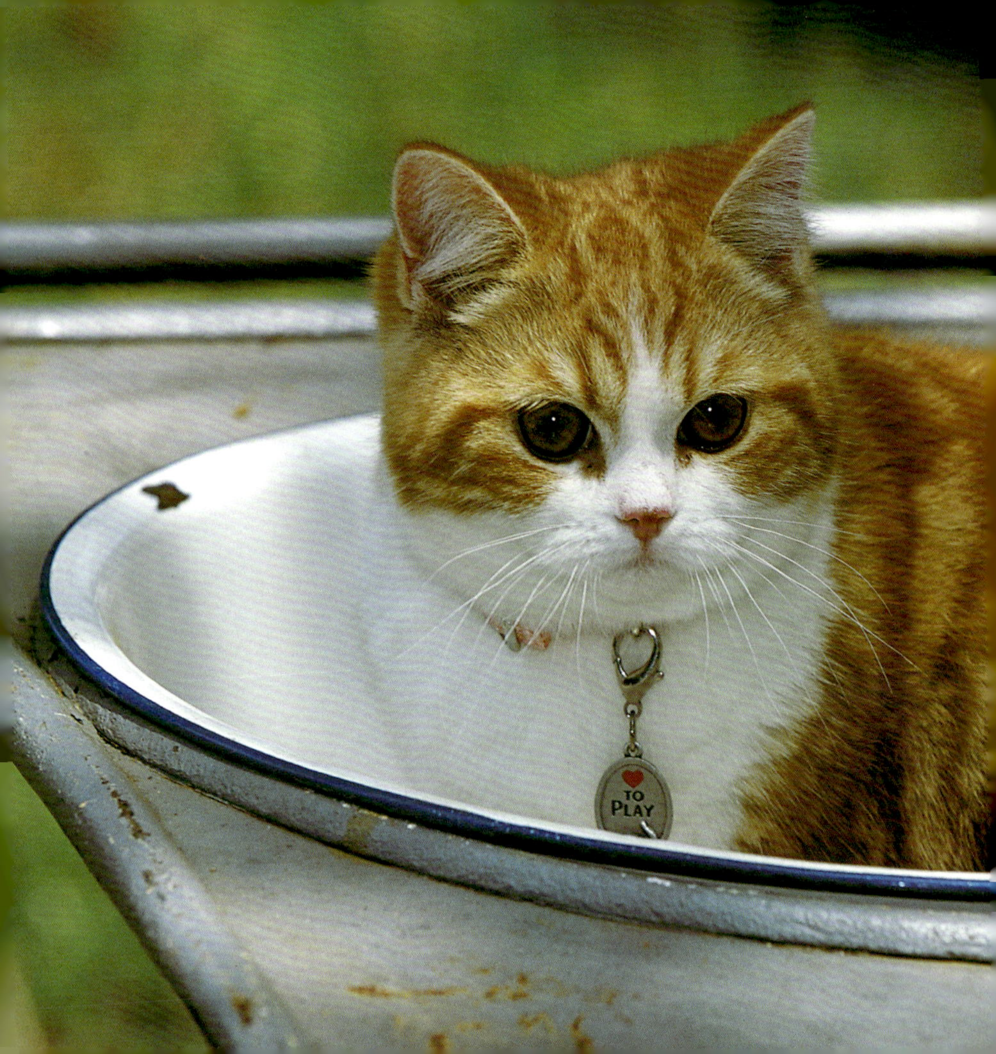
TO
PLAY

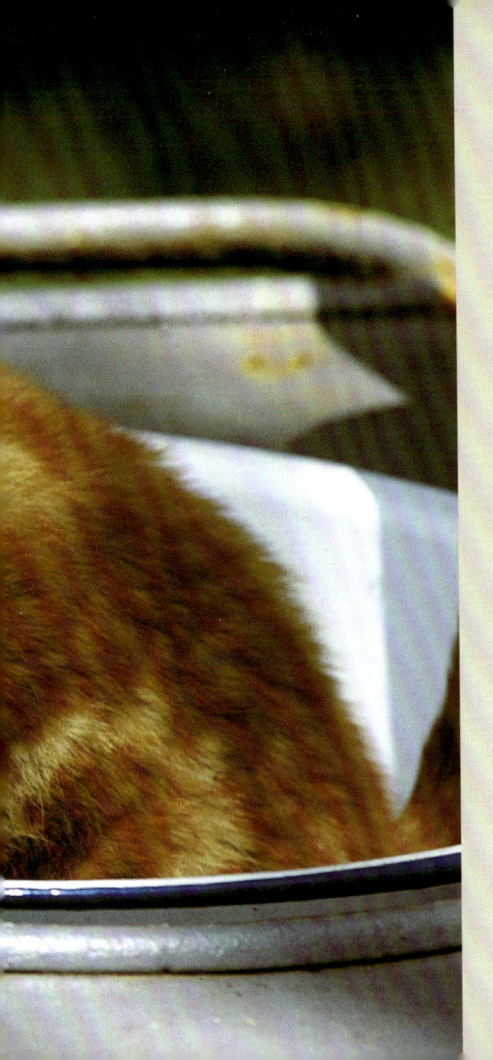

Cats can work out mathematically the *exact place* to sit that will *cause* most *inconvenience*.

Pam Brown

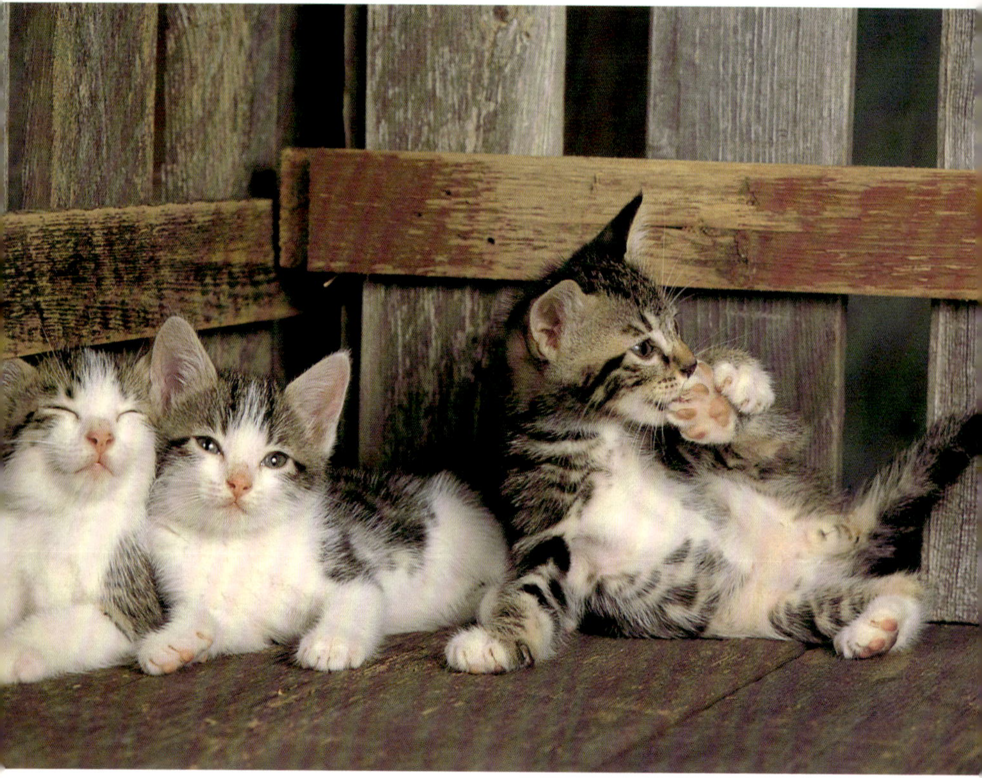

A kitten is so *flexible* that she is almost double; the *hind parts* are equivalent to another kitten with which the *forepart* plays. She does not discover that her *tail* belongs to *her* until you tread on it.

Henry David Thoreau

A cat sees *us* as *dogs*. A cat sees *himself* as a *human*.

—✦—

Anonymous

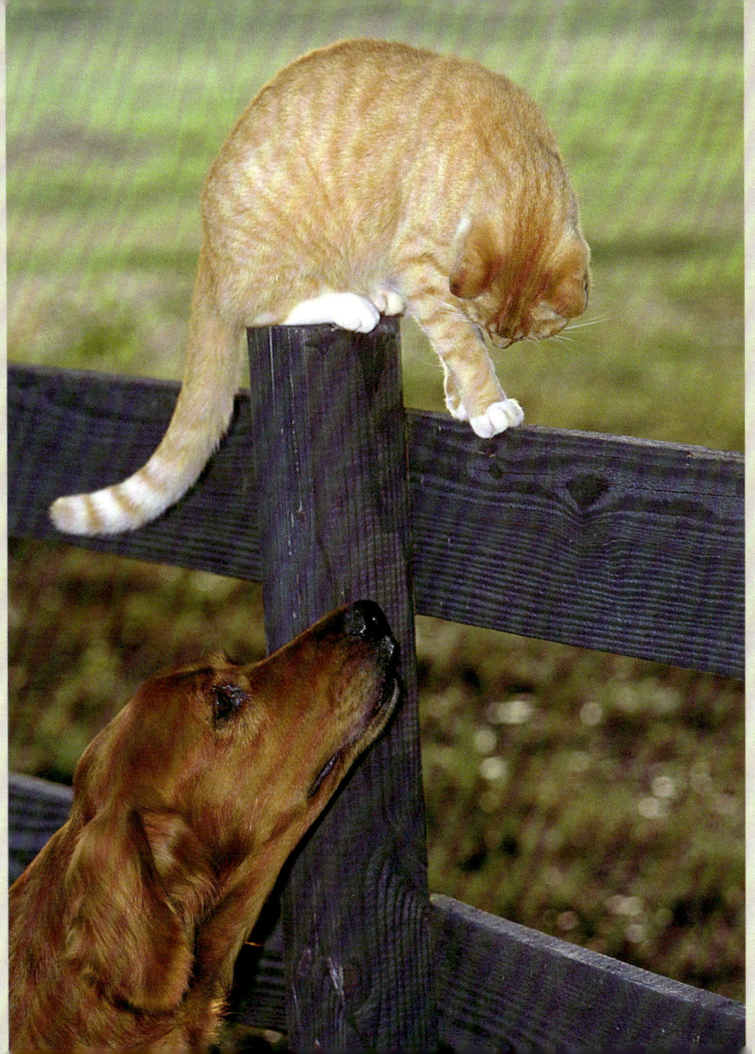

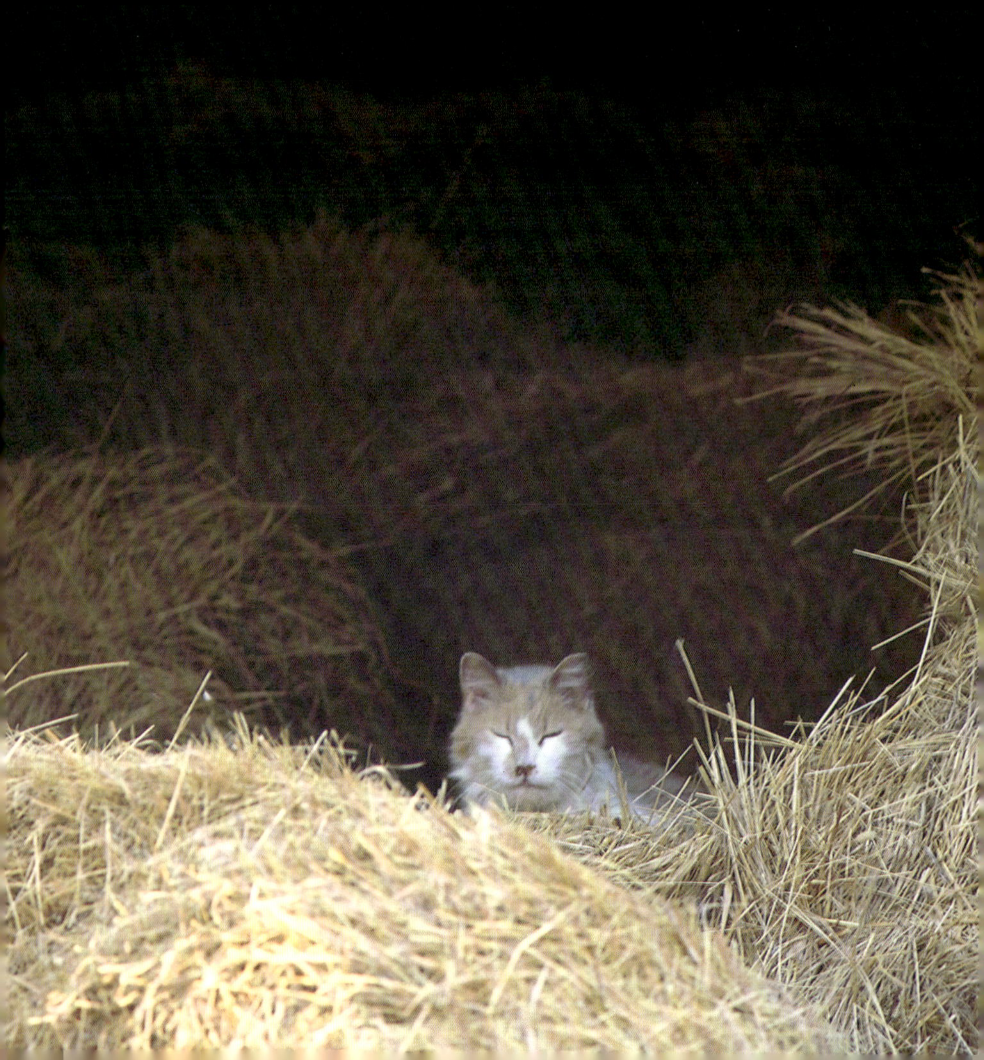

Cats are rather *delicate* creatures and they are subject to a good many *ailments*, but I *never* heard of one who suffered from *insomnia*.

—◆—

Joseph Wood Krutch

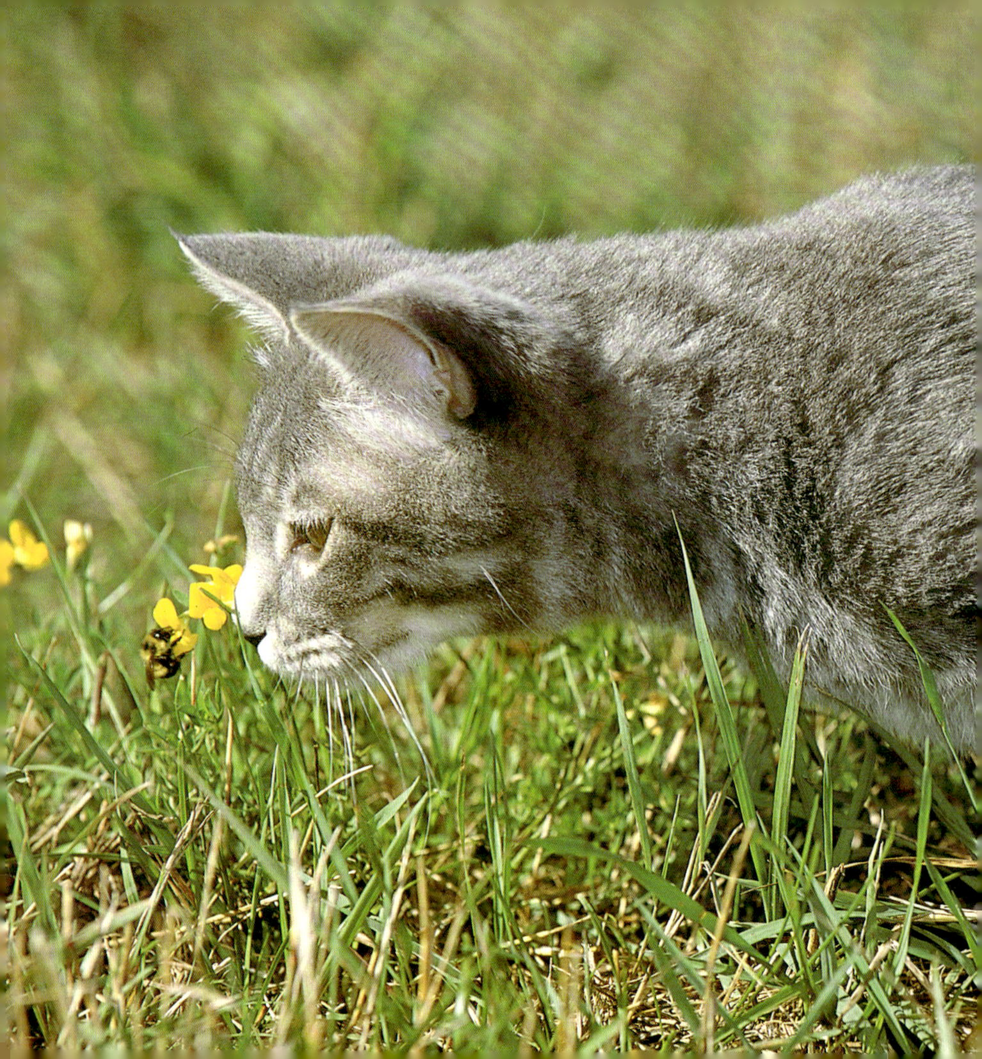

Cats have an *infallible* understanding of total *concentration*—and get between *you* and *it*.

Arthur Bridges

Every cat is *special* in its own way.

—†—

Sara Jane Clark

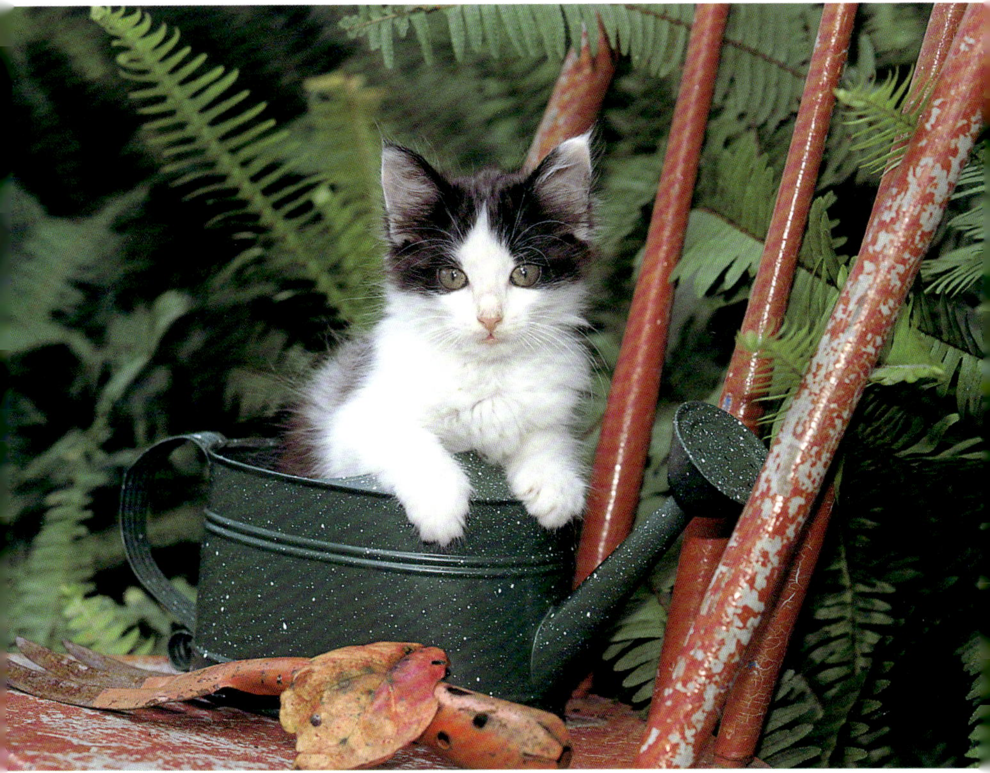

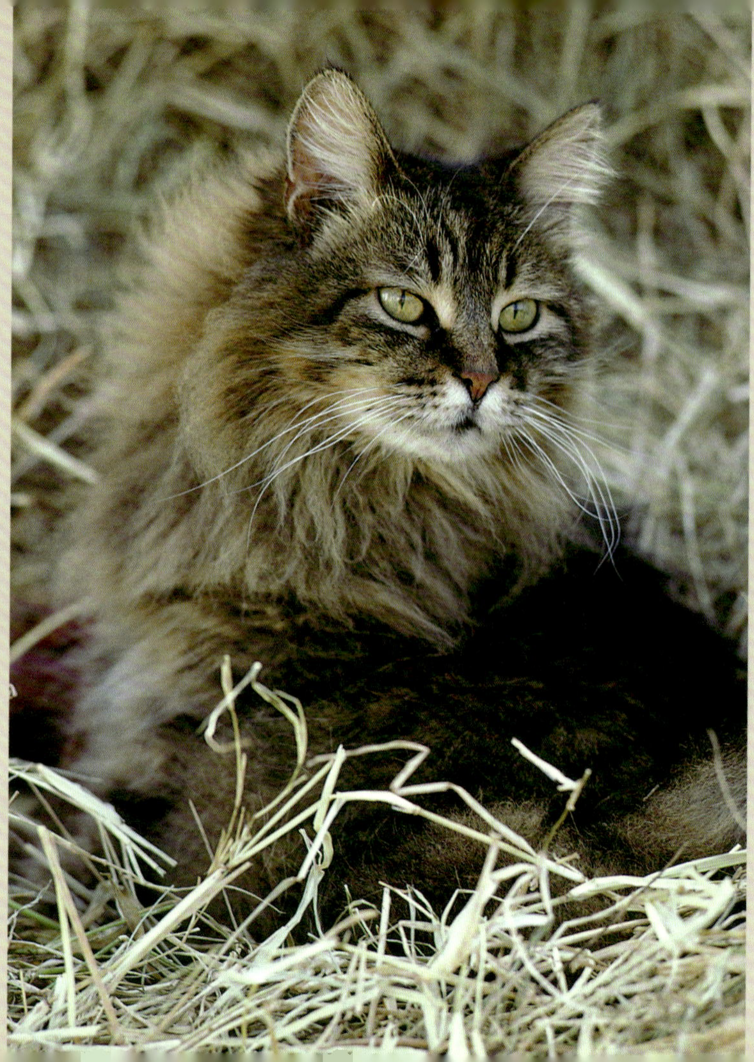

Cats are a *mysterious* kind of folk. There is *more* passing in their *minds* than we are *aware* of.

Sir Walter Scott

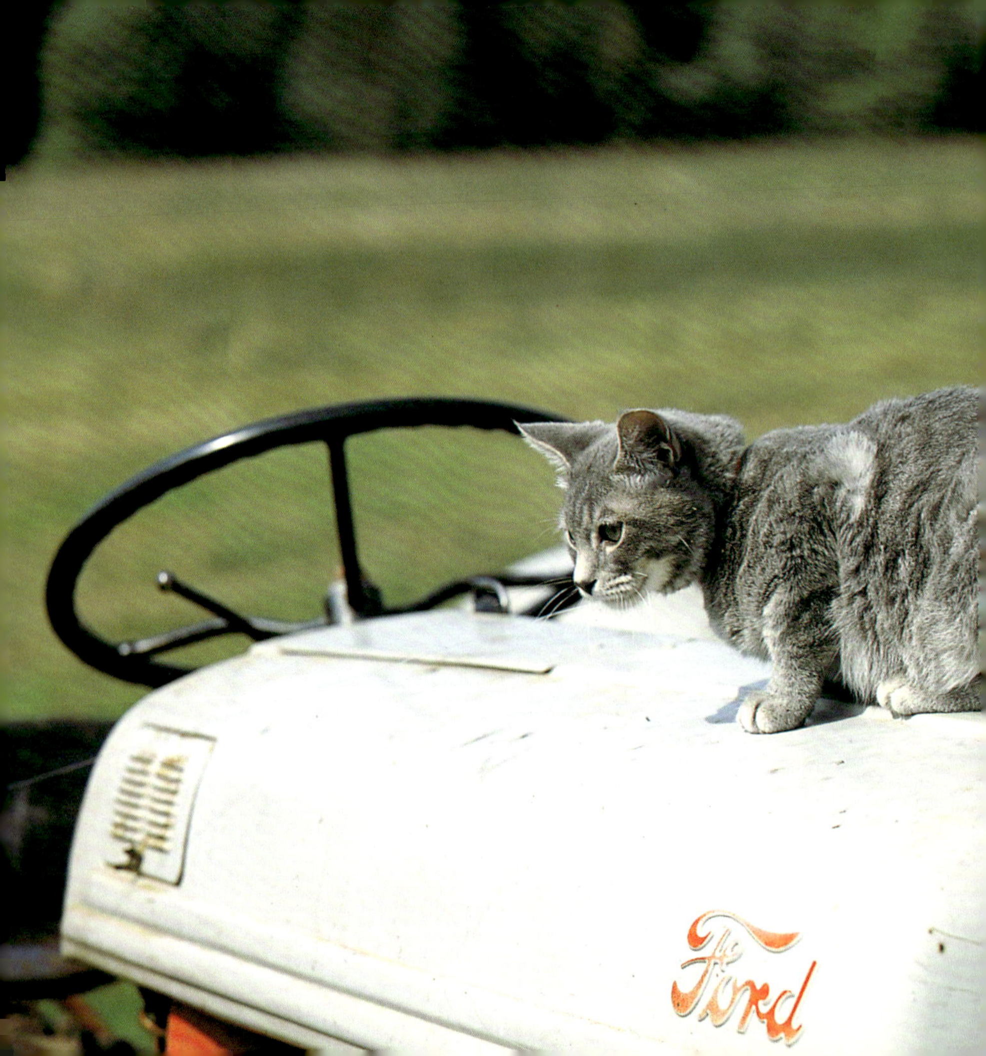
Ford

If *man* could be crossed with the cat it would *improve* man, but it would *deteriorate* the *cat*.

—⊹—

Mark Twain

It is in the *nature* of cats to do a certain amount

of unescorted *roaming*.

—⁌—

Adlai Stevenson

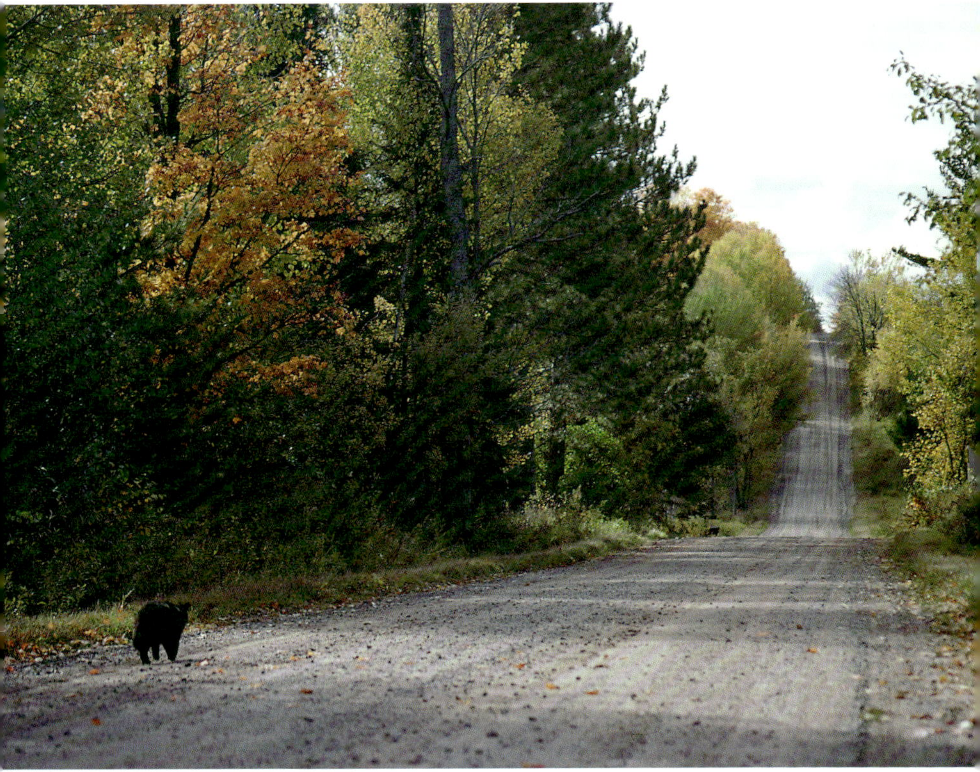

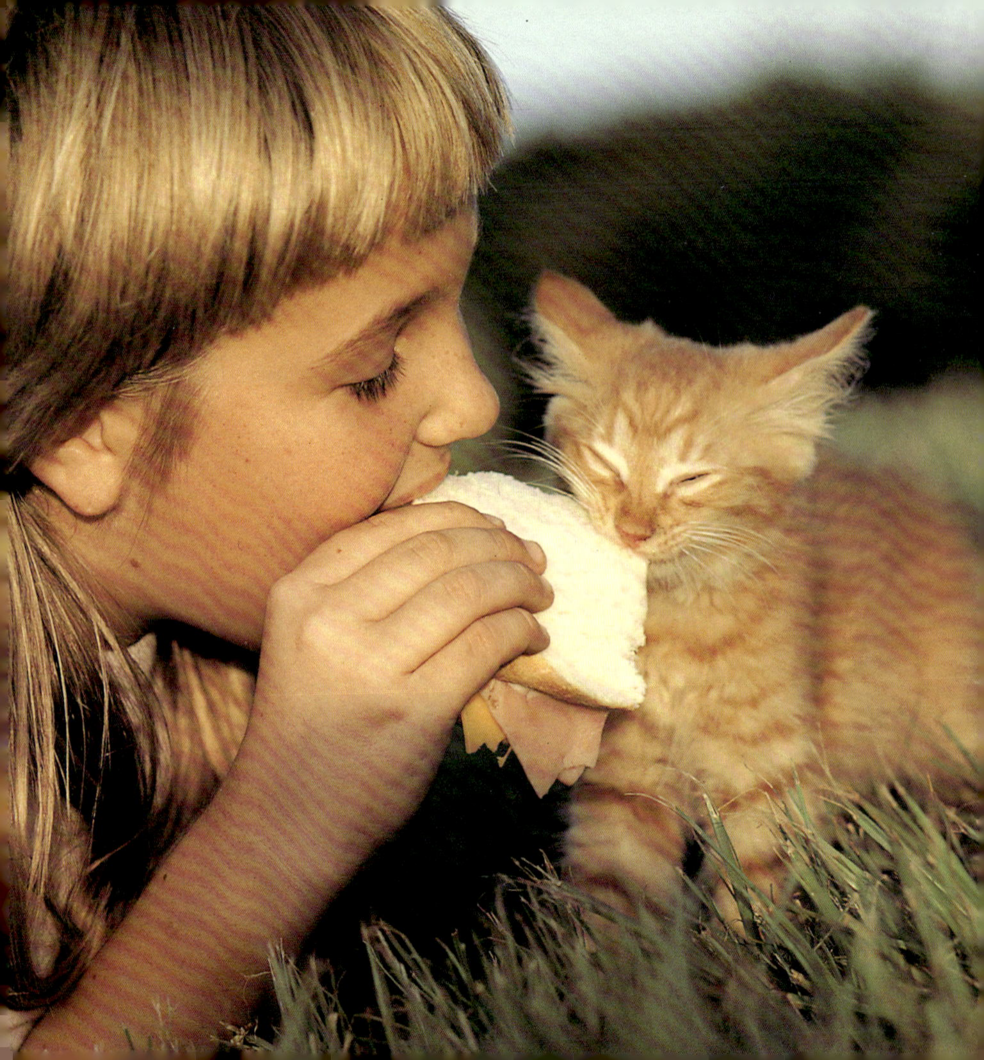

Cats are *designated* friends.

—⊹—

Norman Corwin

People that *hate* cats will come back as *mice* in their next life.

—∗—

Faith Resnick

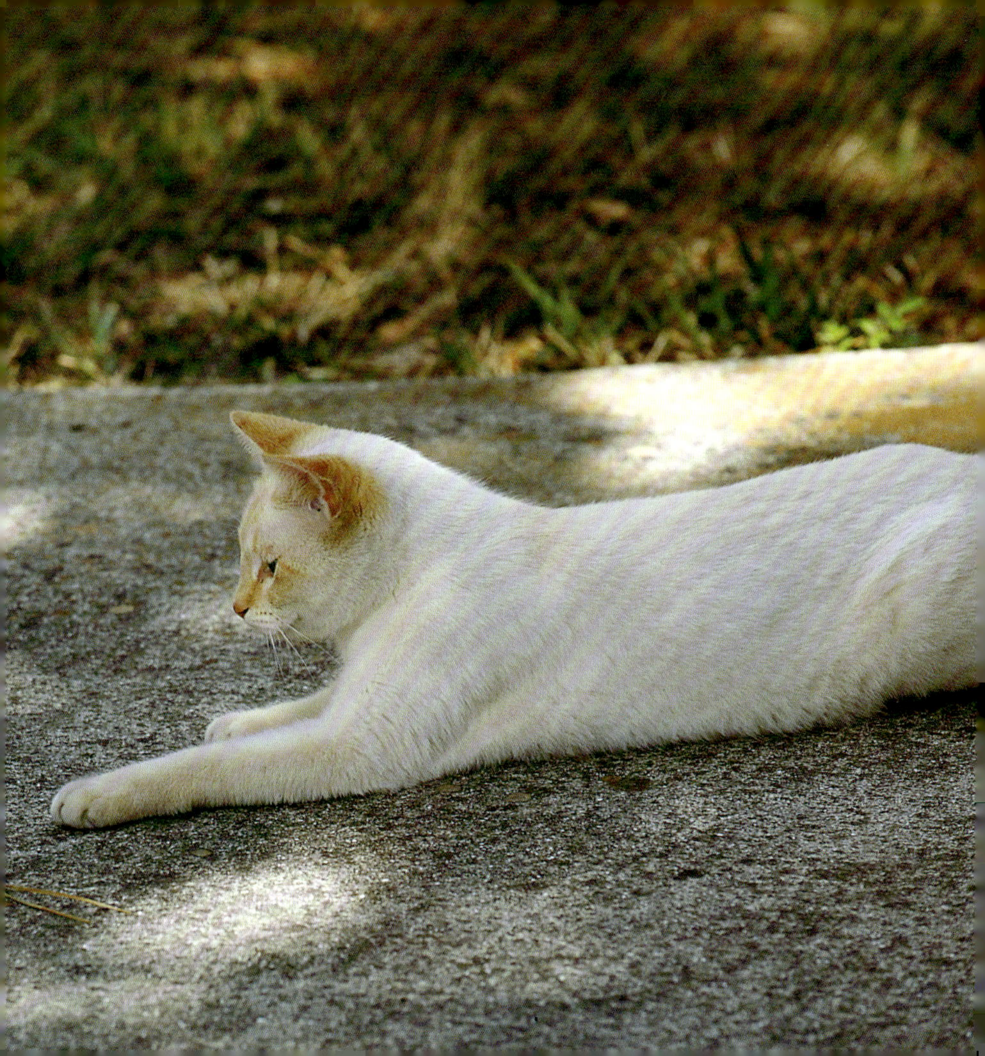

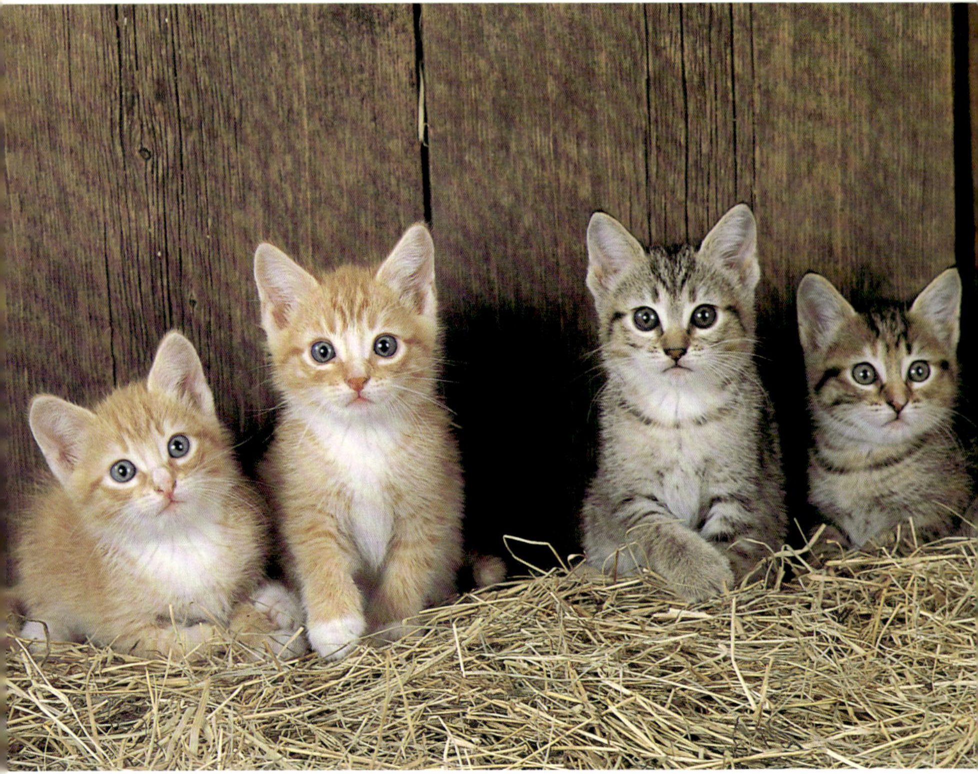

One cat just leads to *another*.

—†—

Ernest Hemingway

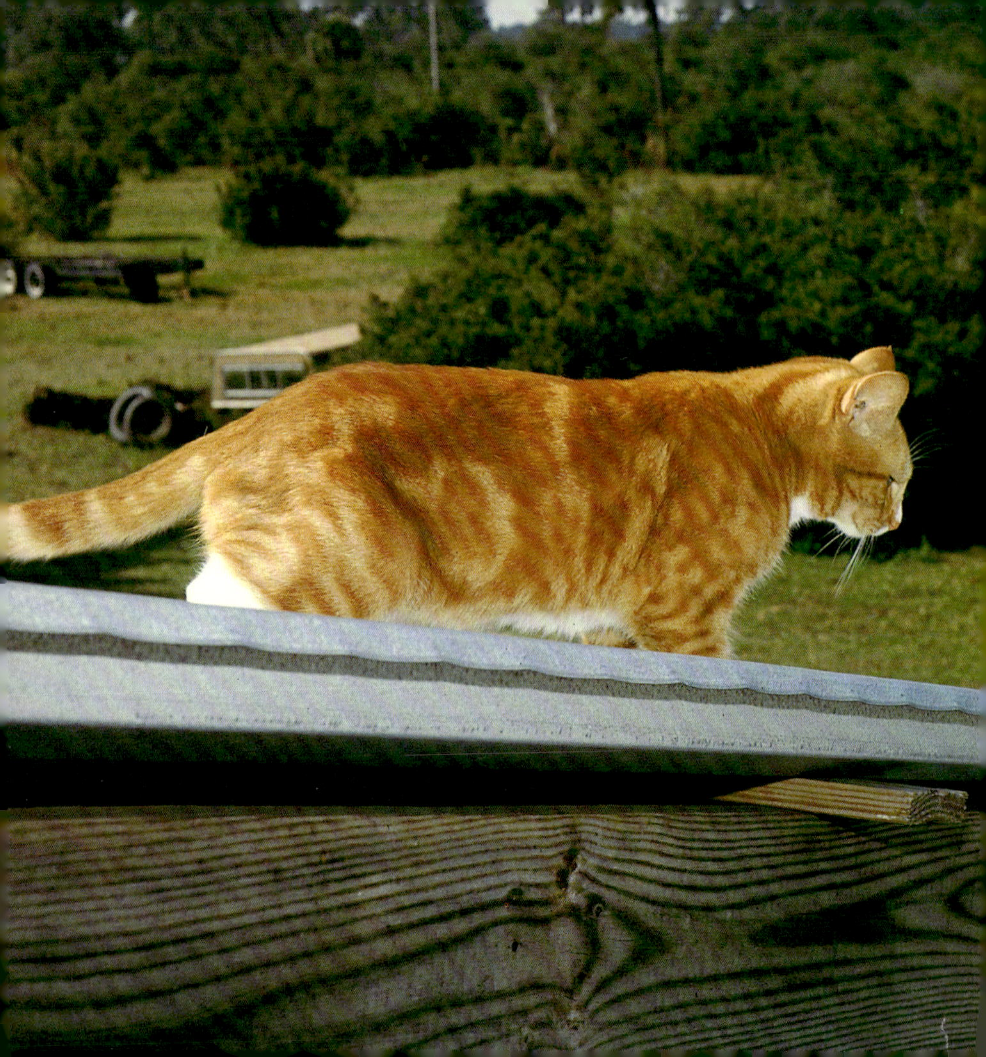

In a cat's eye, *all* things belong to cats.

—⊹—

English Proverb

You can tell your cat *anything* and he'll still *love* you.

If you *lose* your *job* or your *best friend*,

your *cat* will think no less of you.

⁂

Helen Powers

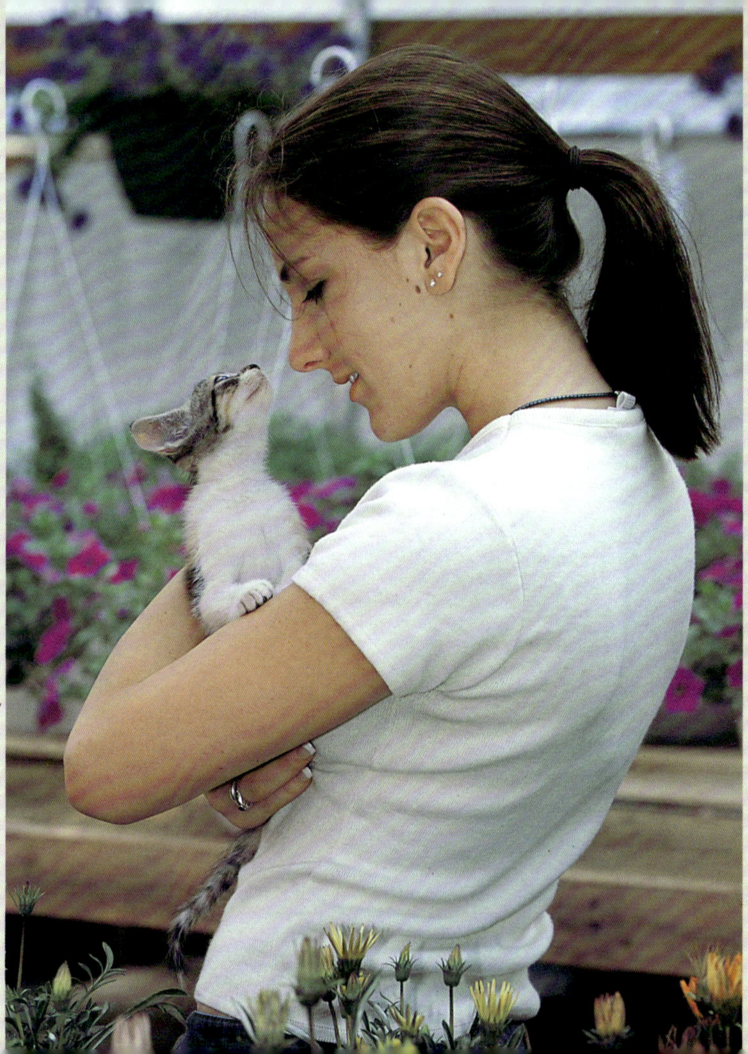

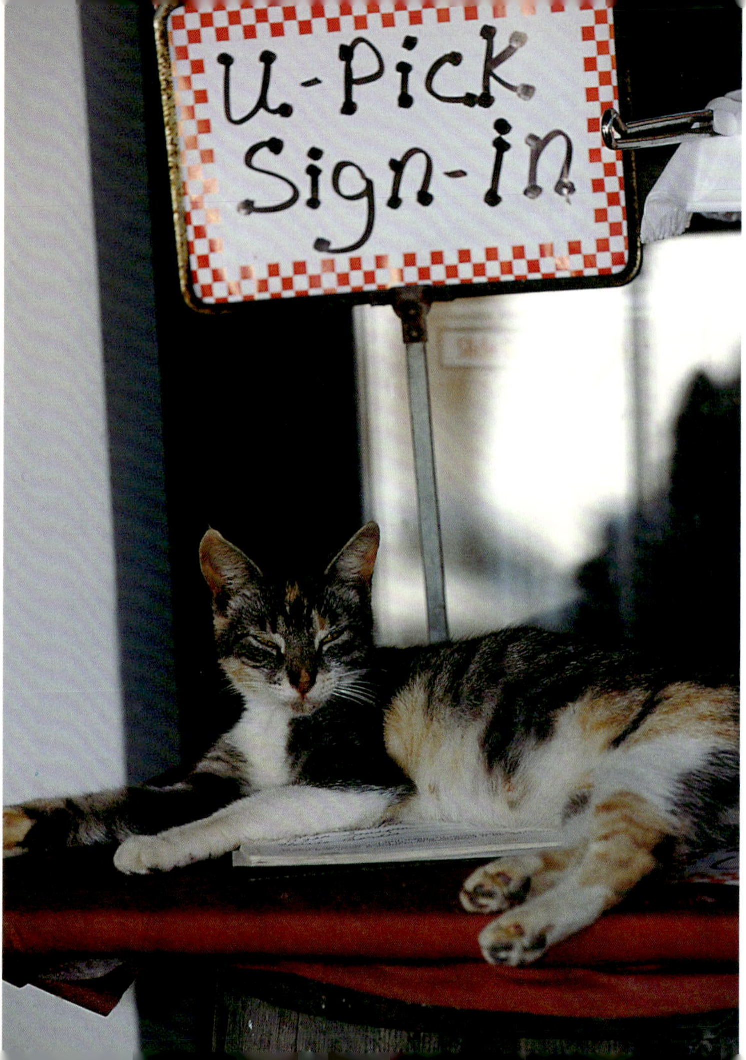
U-Pick
Sign-in

There are *few* things in life more *heartwarming*

than to be *welcomed* by a cat.

—✥—

Tay Hohoff

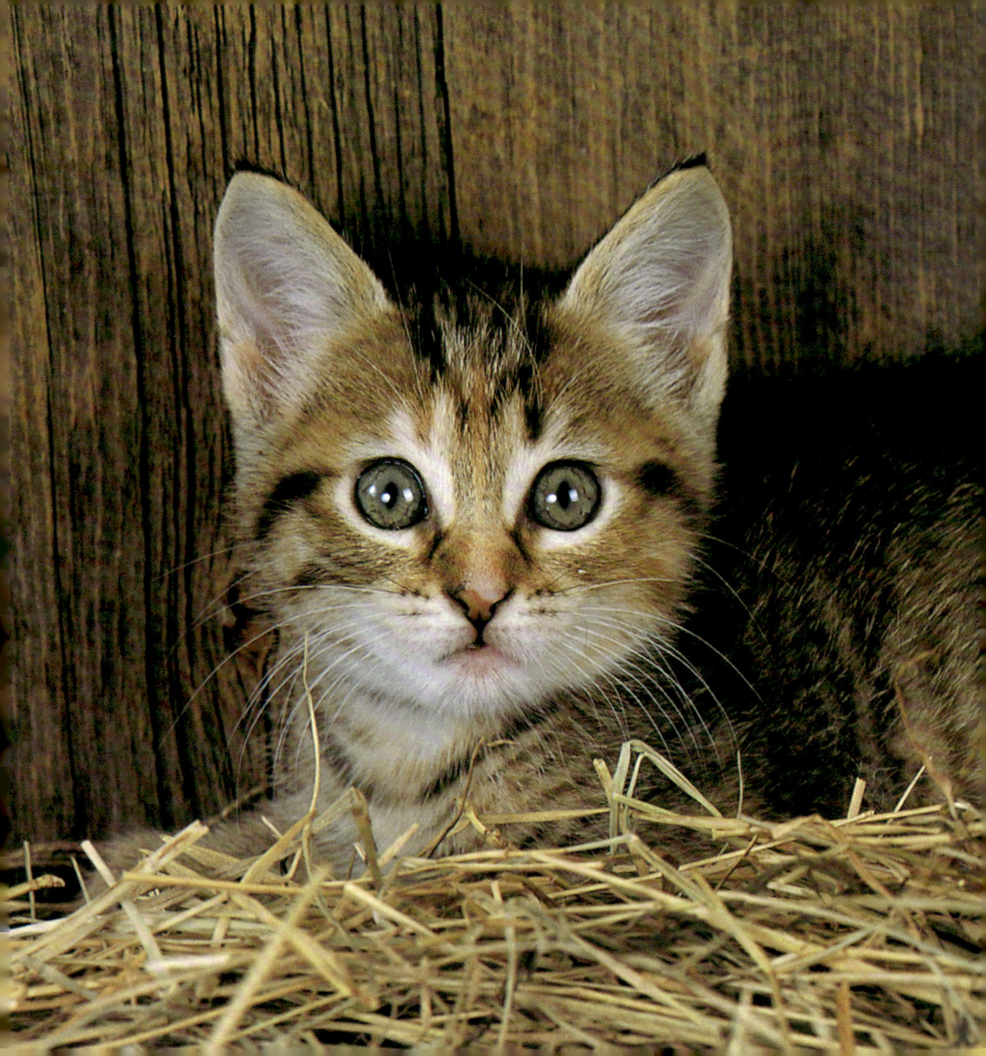

The ideal of *calm* exists

in a sitting cat.

⁌

Jules Renard

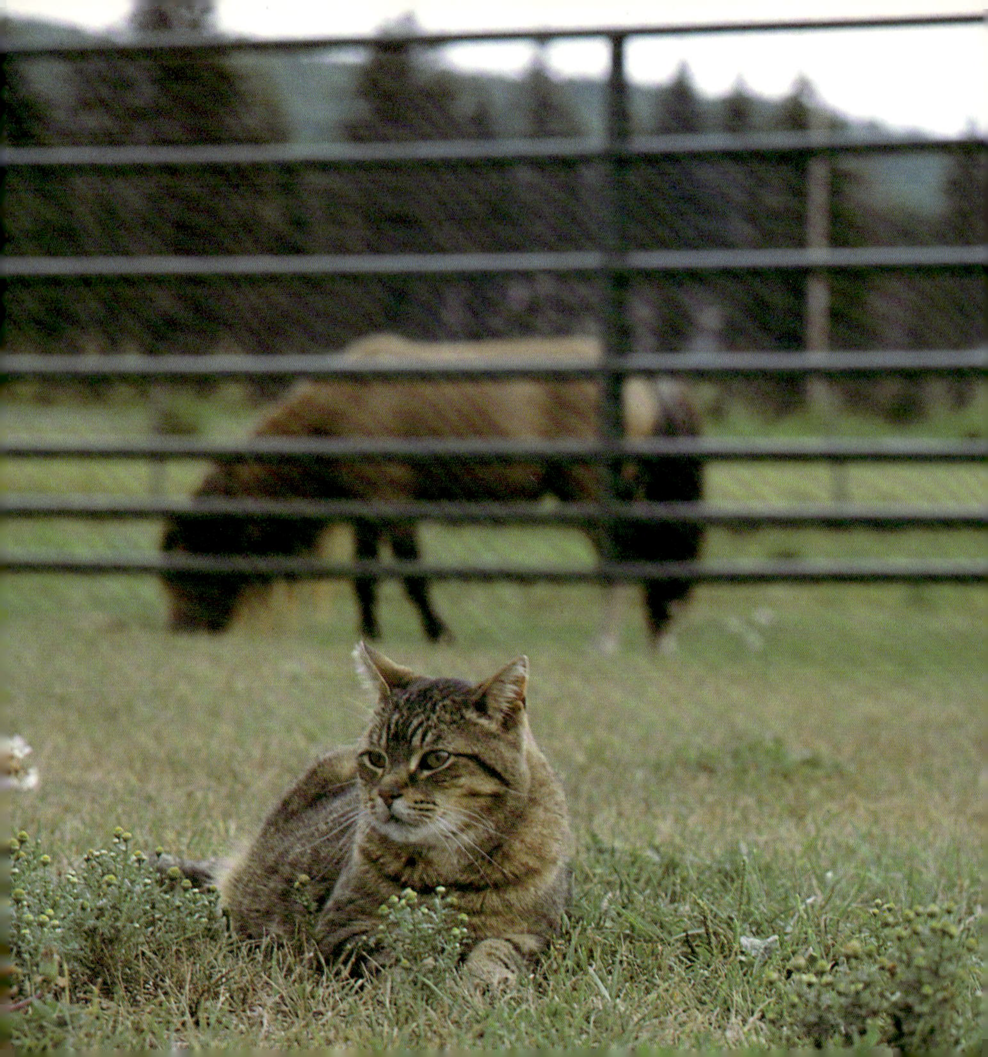

Since *each* of us is blessed with only *one* life, why not

live it with a cat?

—·I·—

Robert Stearns

A little *drowsing* cat is an image of perfect *beatitude*.

—+—

Jules Champfleury

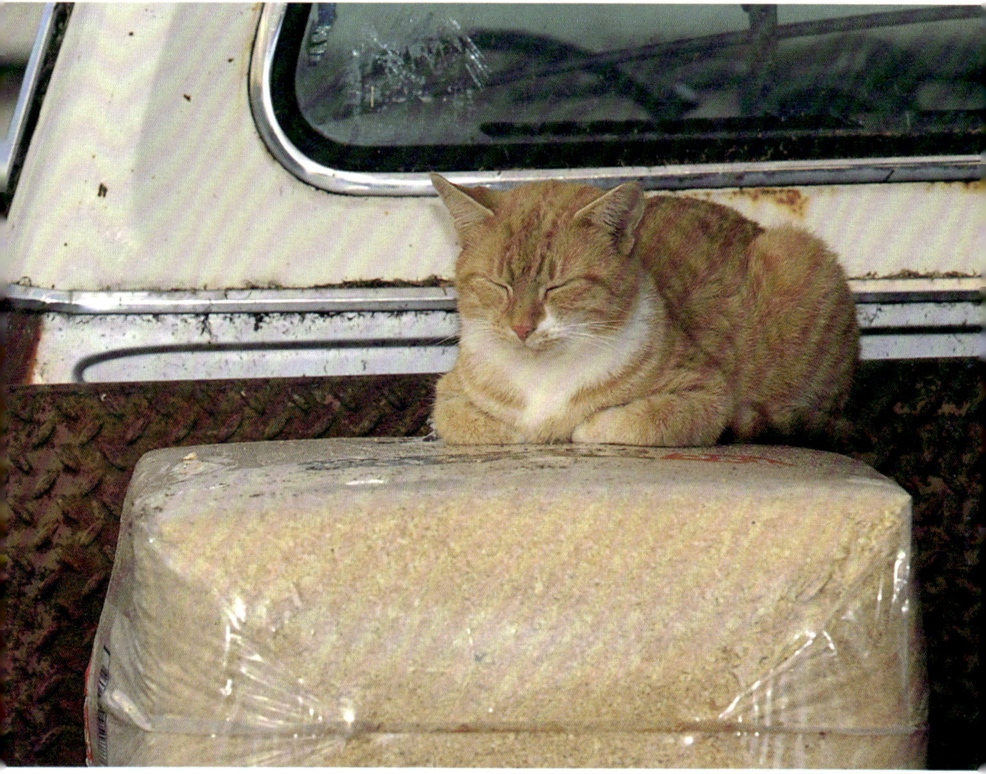

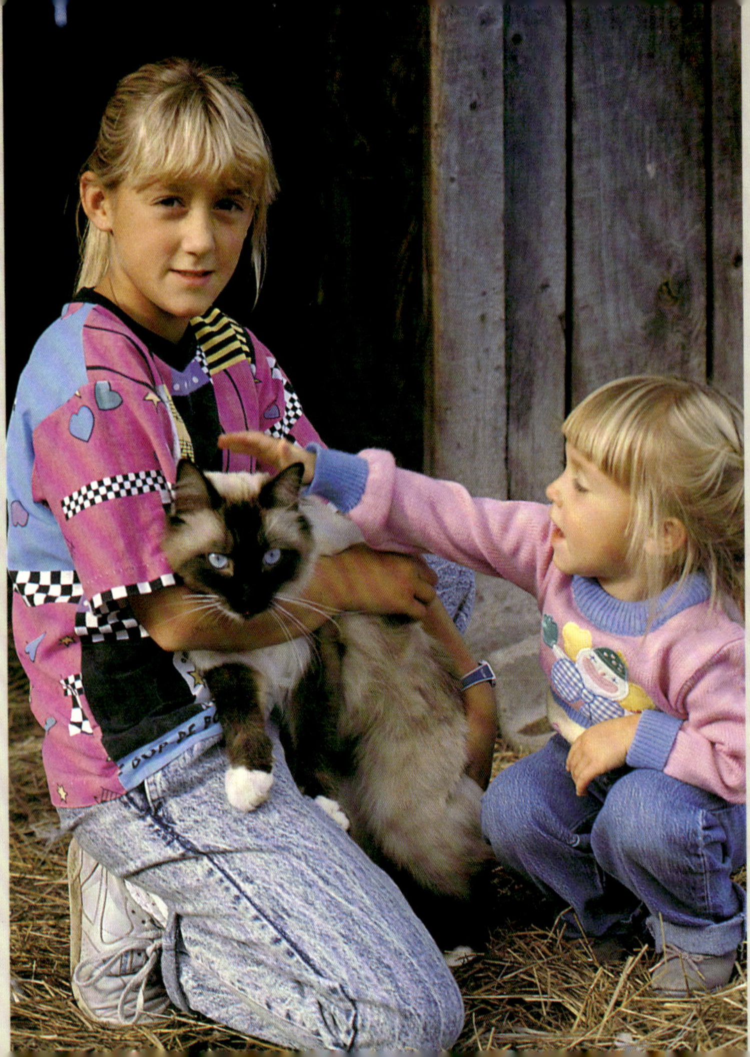

If we treated *everyone* we meet with the same *affection* we bestow upon our favorite *cat*, they, too, would *purr*.

Martin Buxbaum

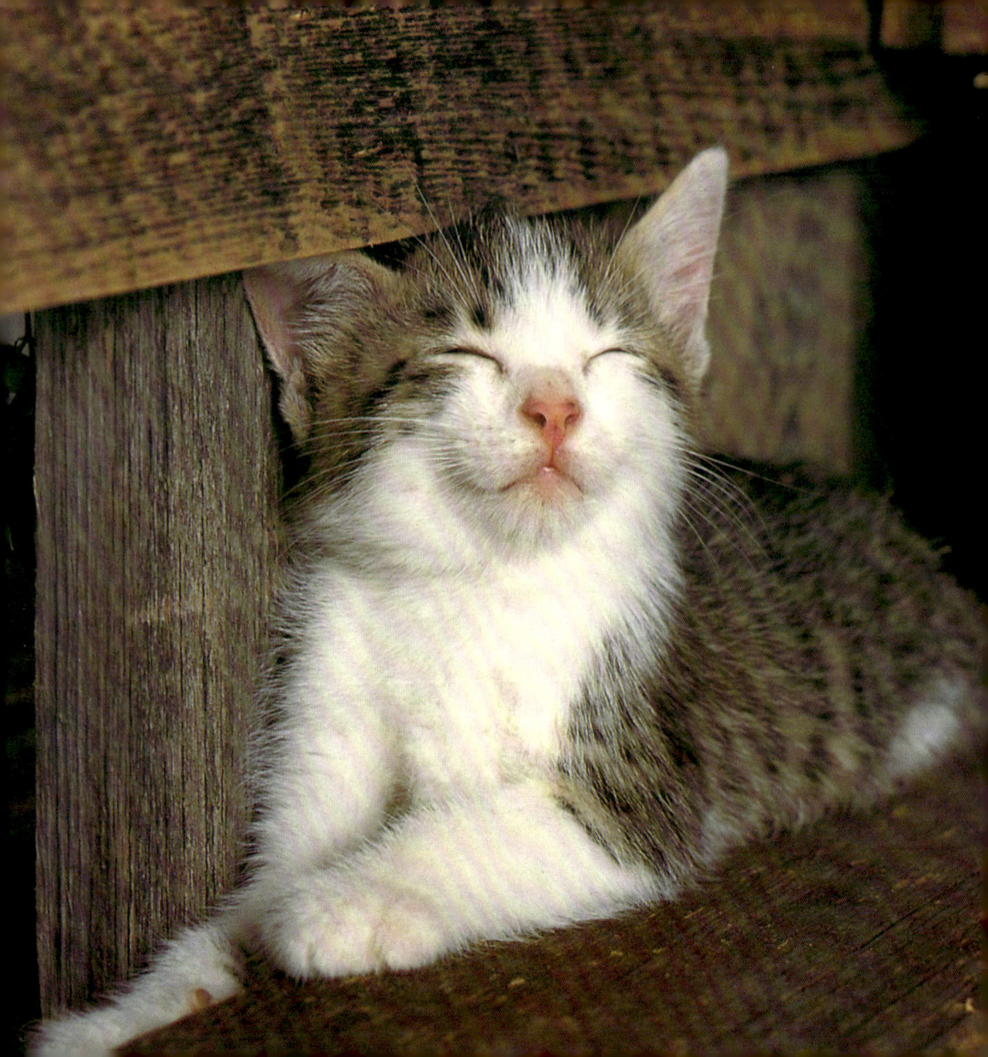

It is a very *convenient* habit

of *kittens* that whatever

you say to them,

they always *purr*.

Lewis Carroll

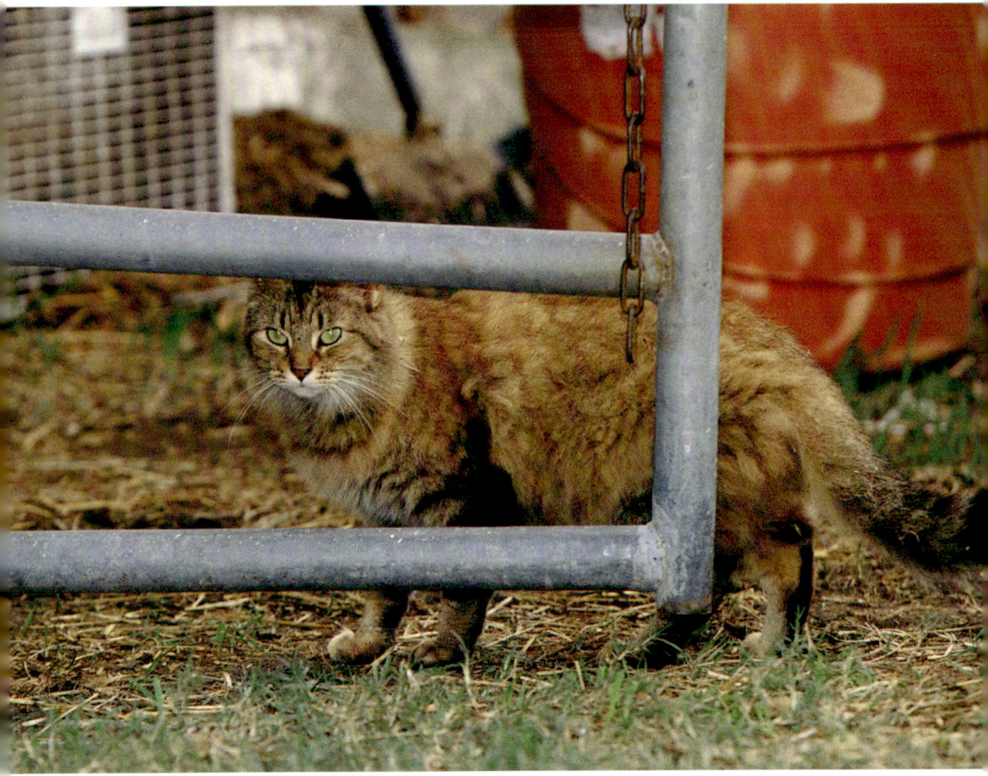

If the *pull* of the outside world is strong,

there is also a pull towards the *human*. The cat may

disappear on its own errands, but sooner or later,

it *returns* once again for a little while, to *greet* us

with its own type of *love*. Independent as they are,

cats find more than pleasure in *our* company.

Lloyd Alexander

A cat has *absolute* emotional honesty. Human beings,

for one reason or another, may *hide* their feelings,

but a cat does *not*.

— I —

Ernest Hemingway

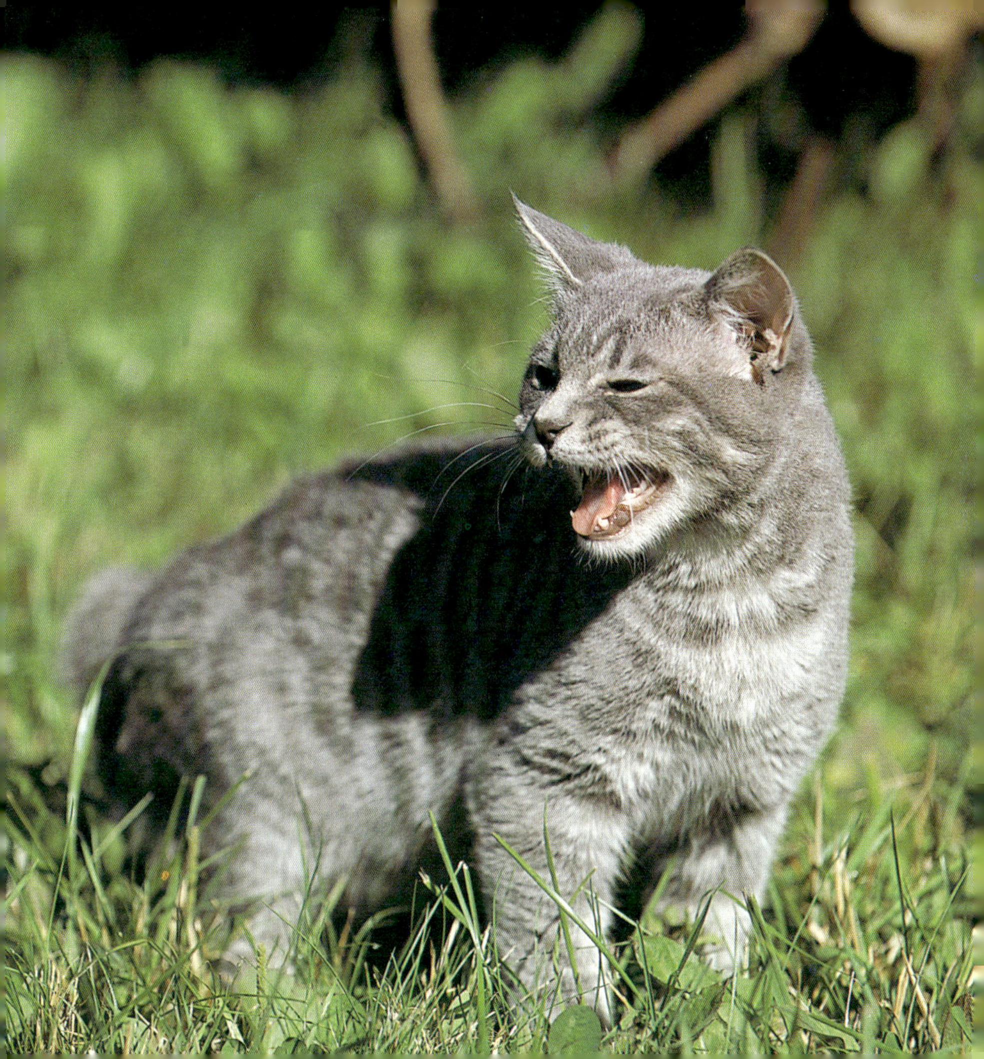

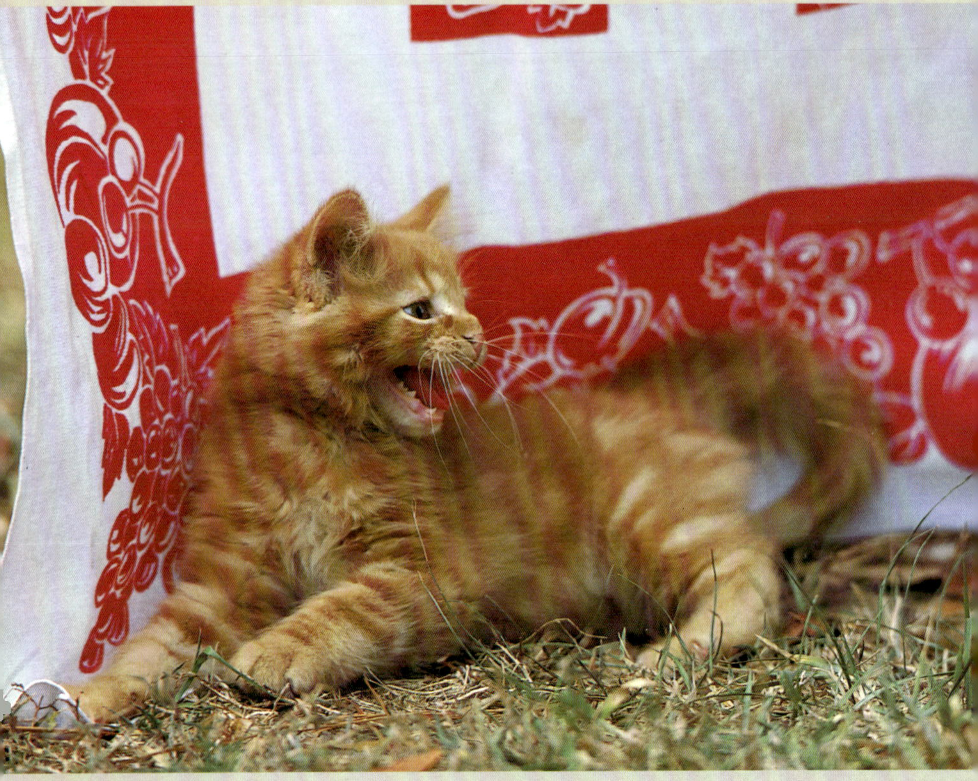

A meow *massages* the heart.

Stuart McMillan

Cats do not have to be *shown* how to have a good time, for they are unfailing *ingenious* in that respect.

James Mason

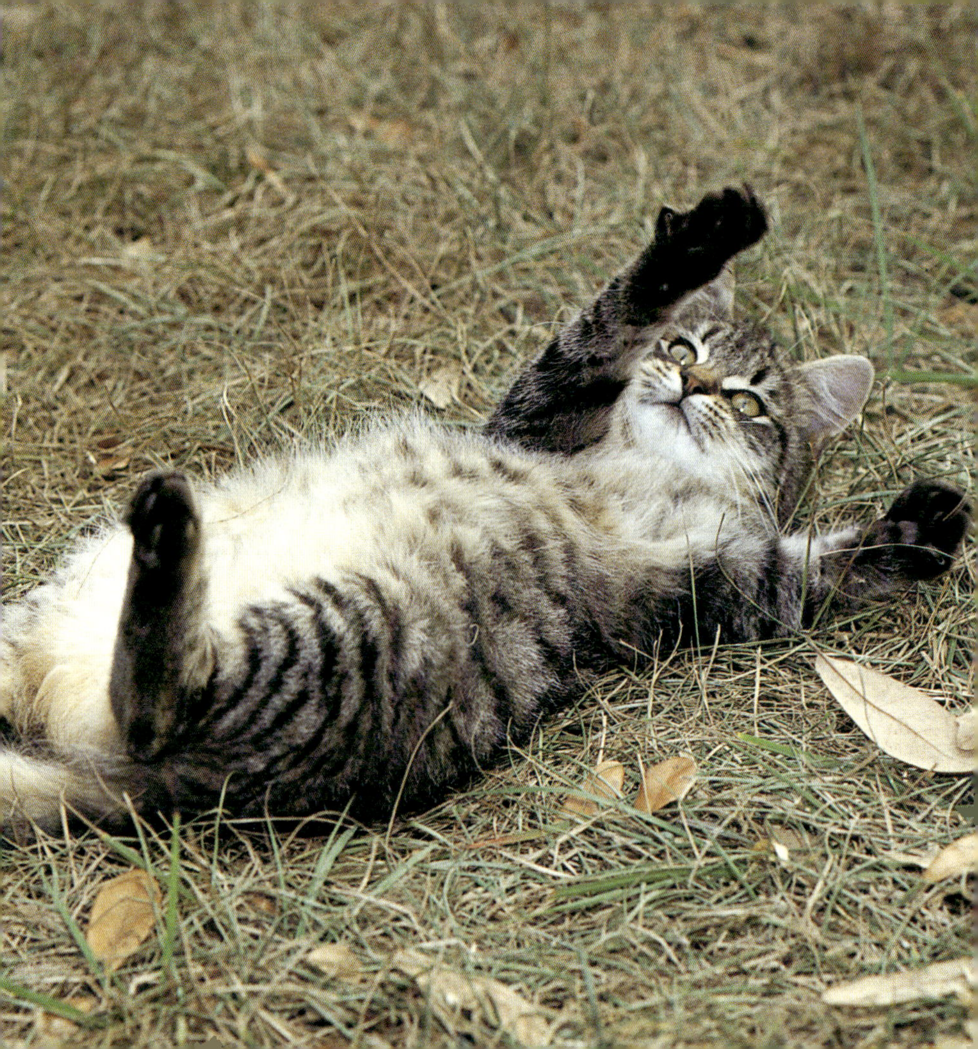

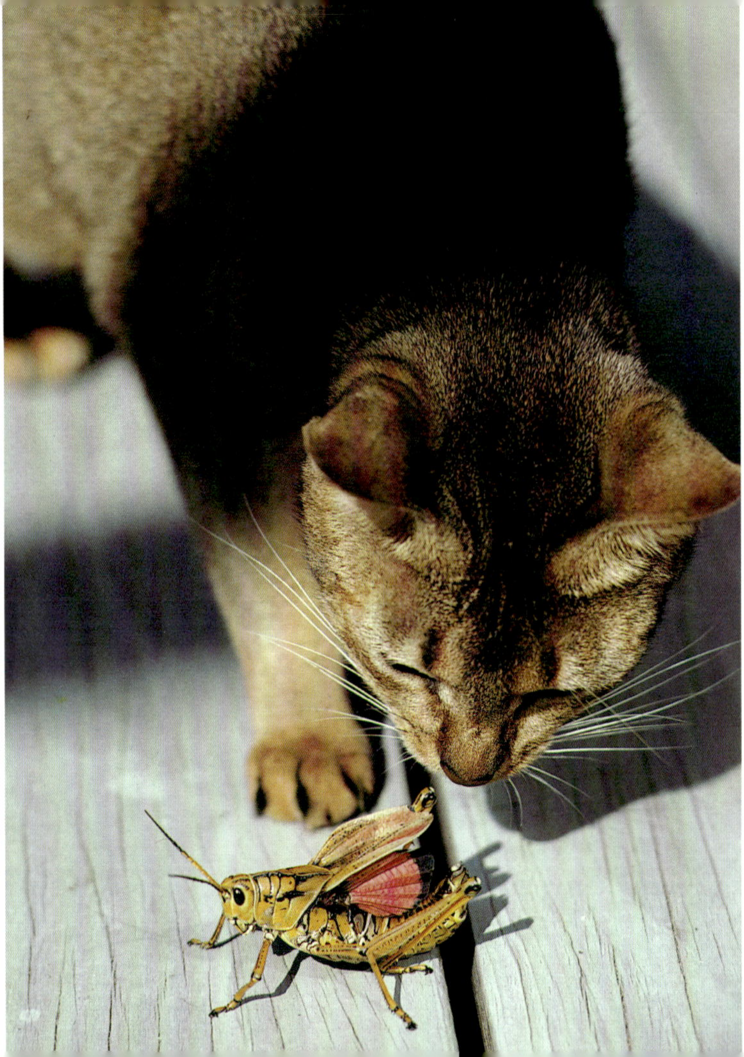

I *wish* I could write as *mysterious* as a cat.

—I—

Edgar Allan Poe

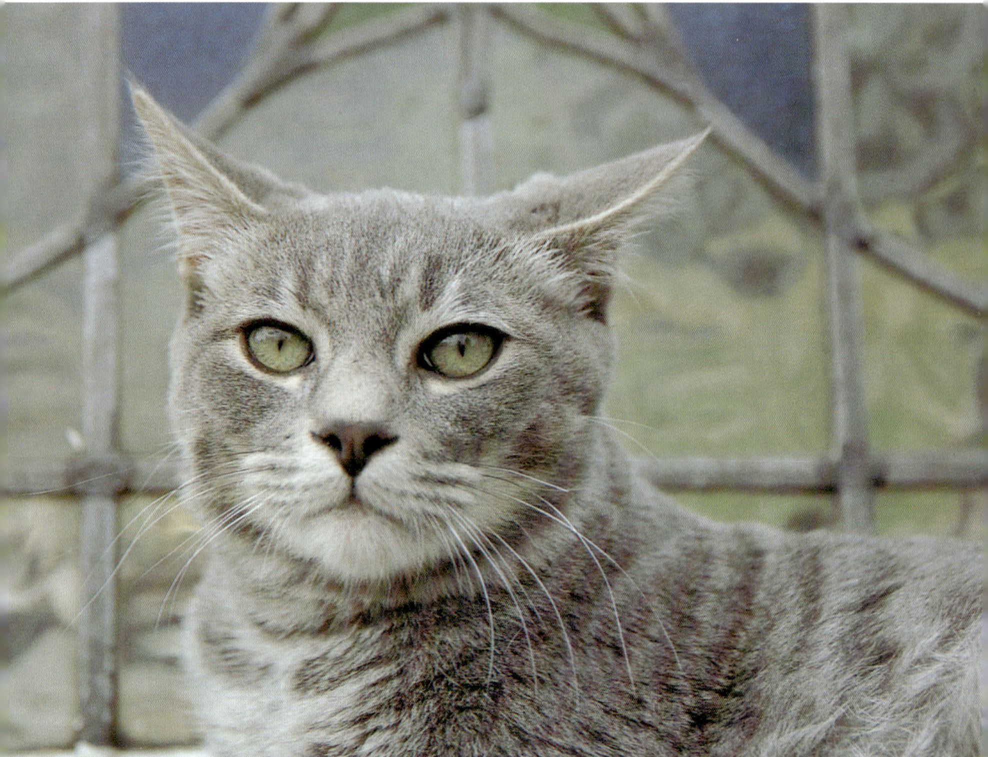

Way down deep, we're all *motivated* by the same urges. Cats have the *courage* to live by them.

—⁕—

Jim Davis

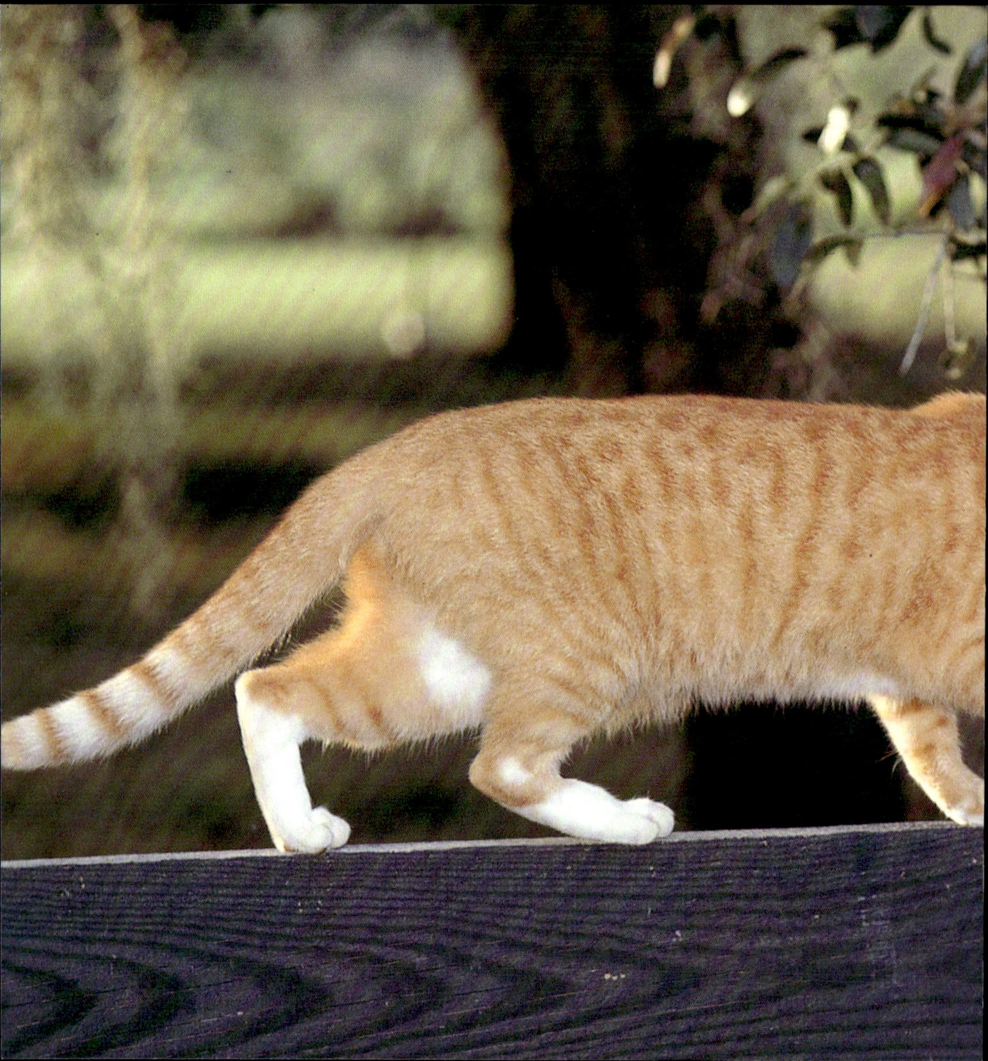

As *every* cat owner knows,

nobody owns a cat.

Ellen Perry
Berkeley

Do you see that kitten *chasing* so prettily her own tail? If you could *look* with her eyes, you might see her *surrounded* with hundreds of figures *performing* complex dramas, with tragic and comic issues, *long* conversations, many characters, many *ups* and *downs* of fate.

Ralph Waldo Emerson

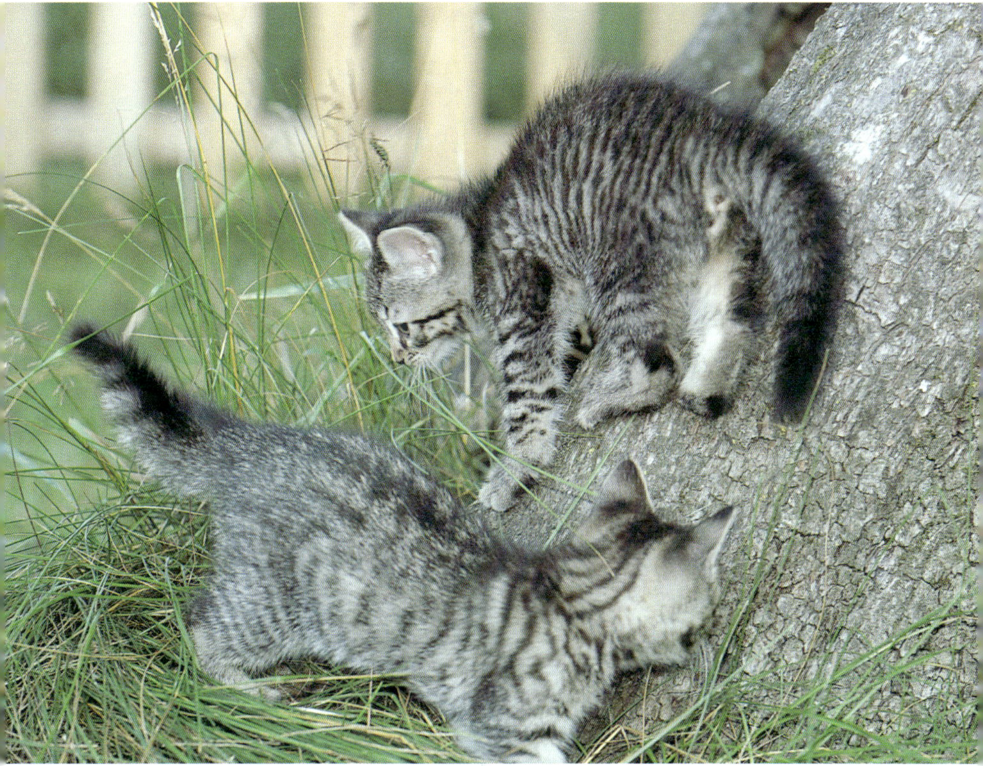

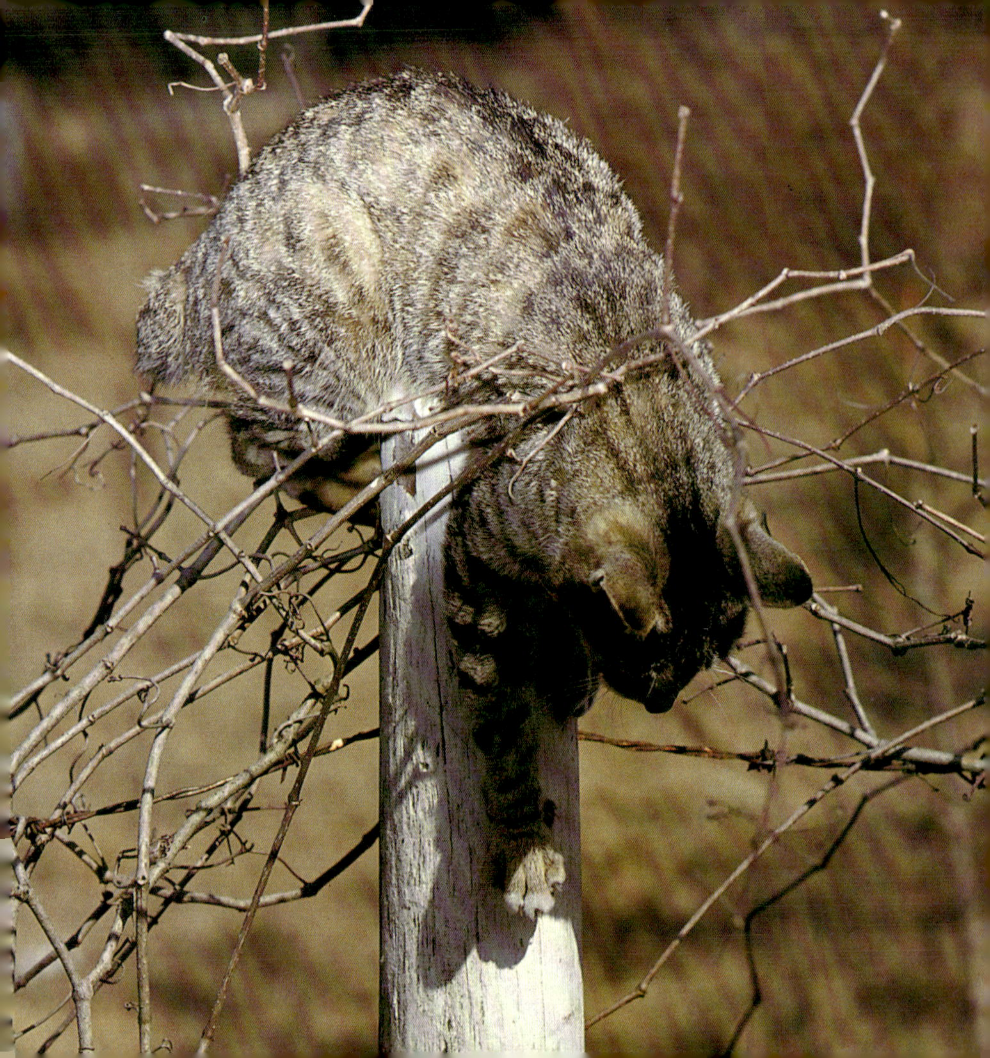

I believe cats to be *spirits* come to earth.

A cat, I am sure, could *walk* on a cloud

without coming through.

Jules Verne

There are no *ordinary* cats.

—❧—

Colette

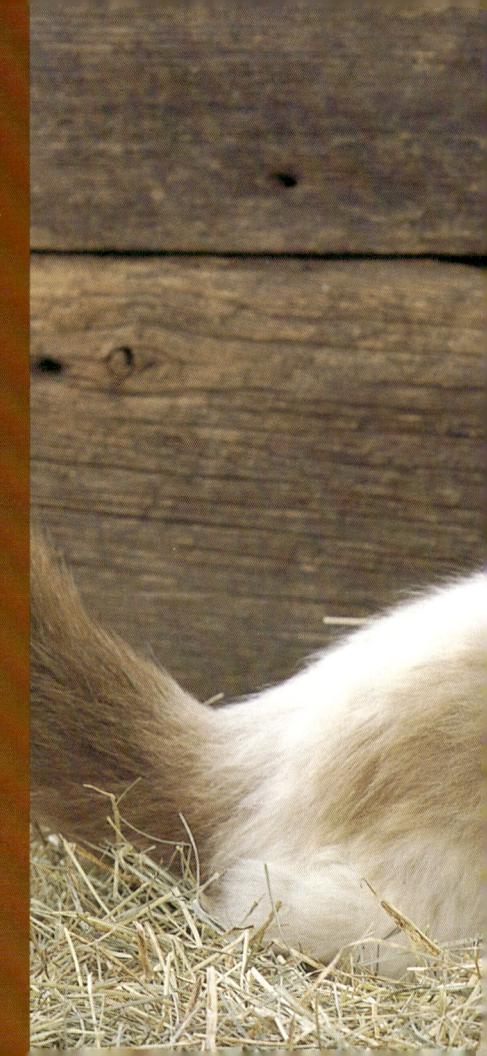

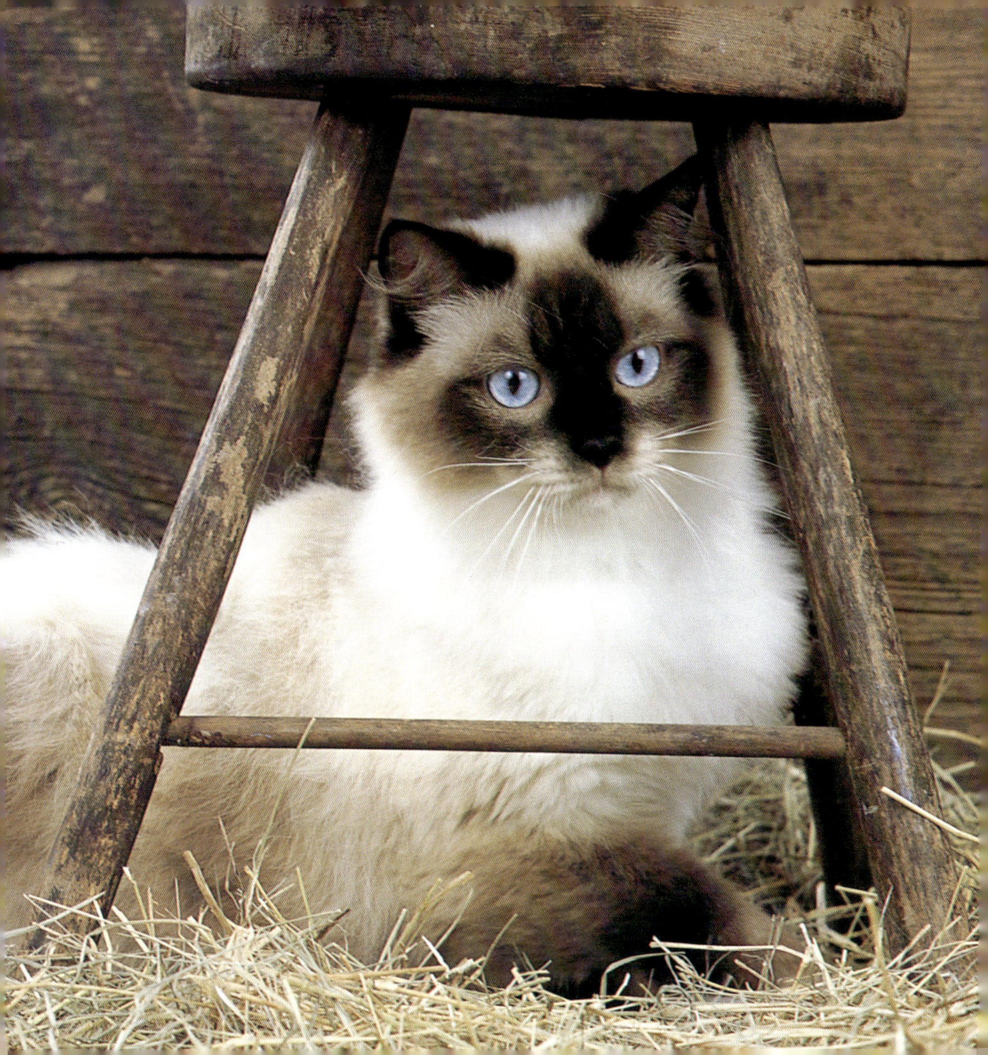

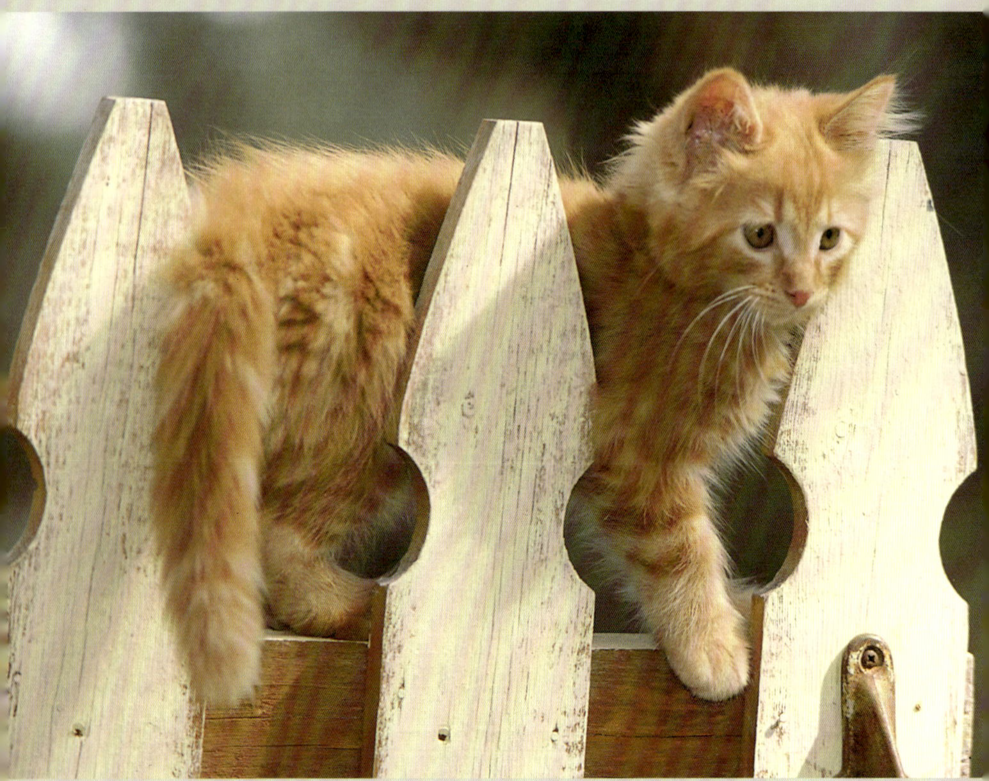

A kitten is chiefly *remarkable* for rushing about

like mad at *nothing* whatever,

and generally *stopping* before it gets there.

Agnes Repplier

Like a *graceful* vase, a cat, even when *motionless*,

seems to *flow*.

⊷I⊶

George F. Will

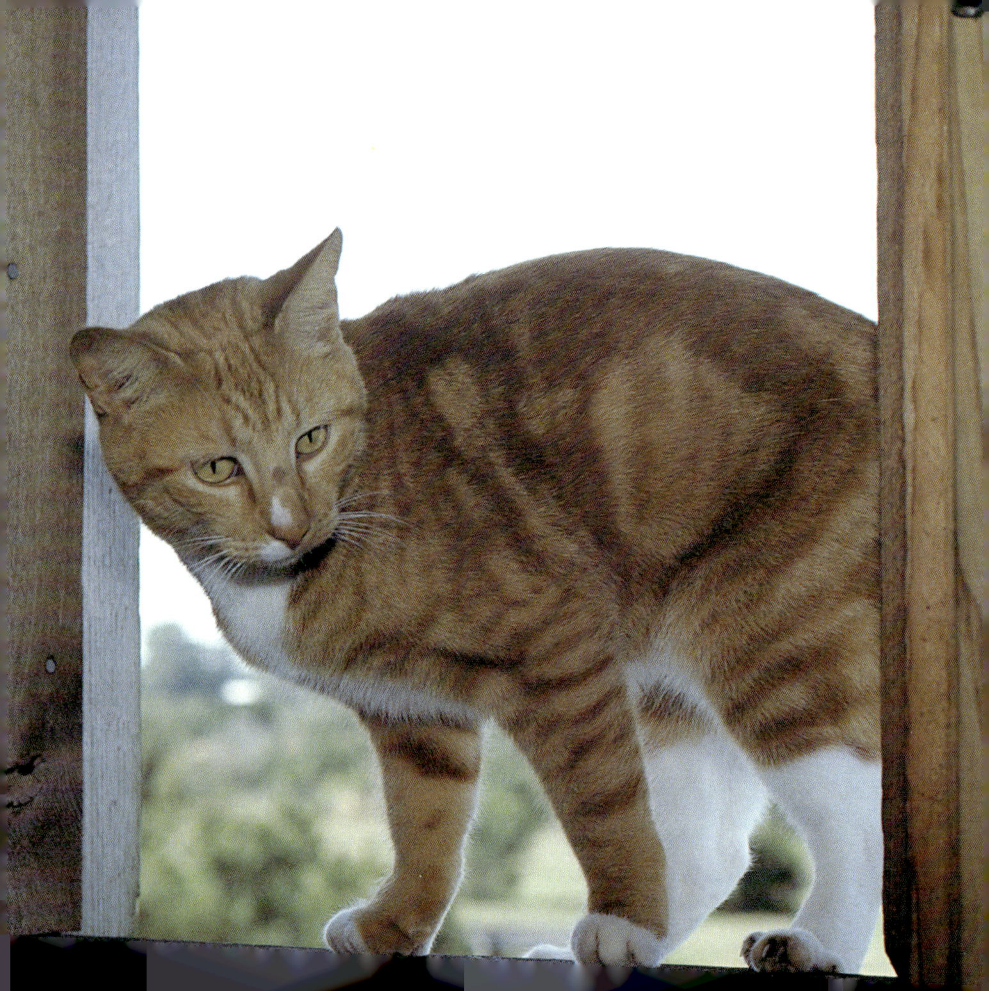

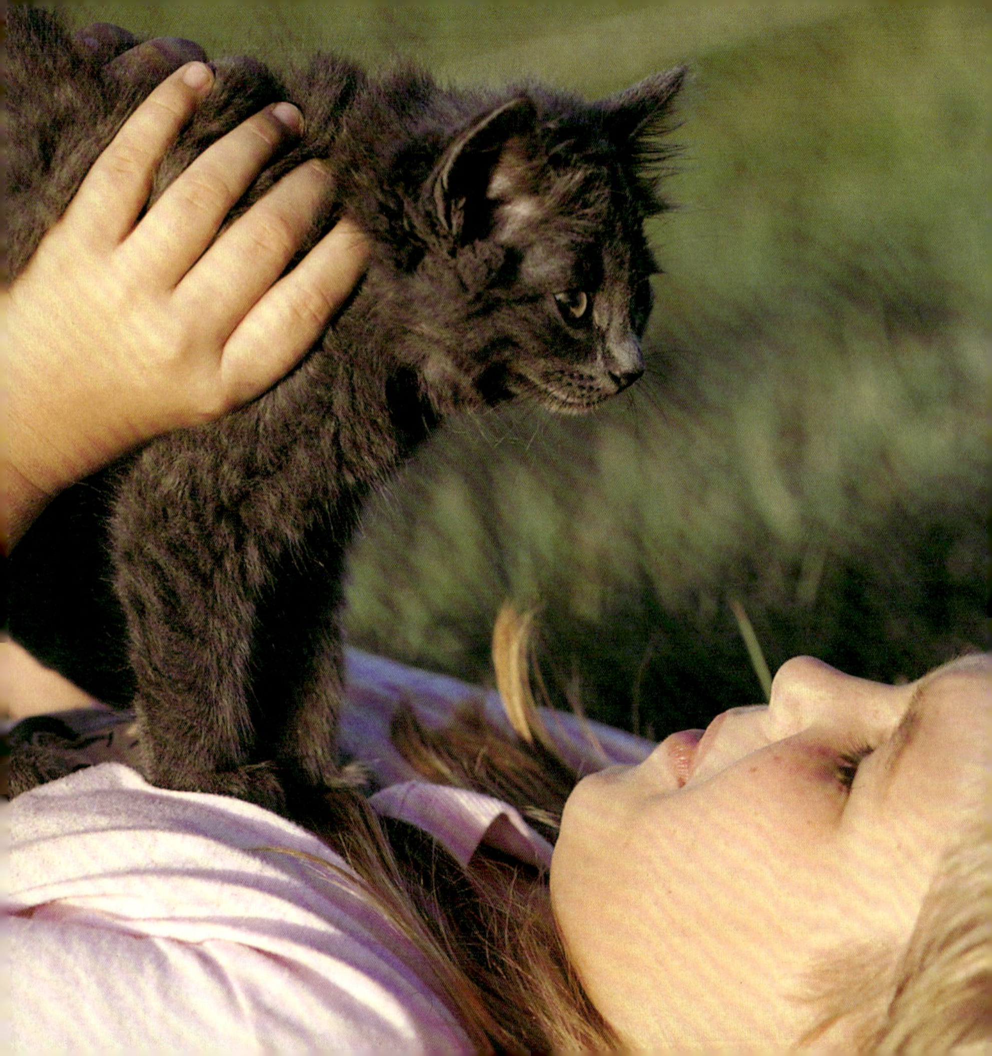

Time spent with cats

is *never wasted.*

⸹

Colette

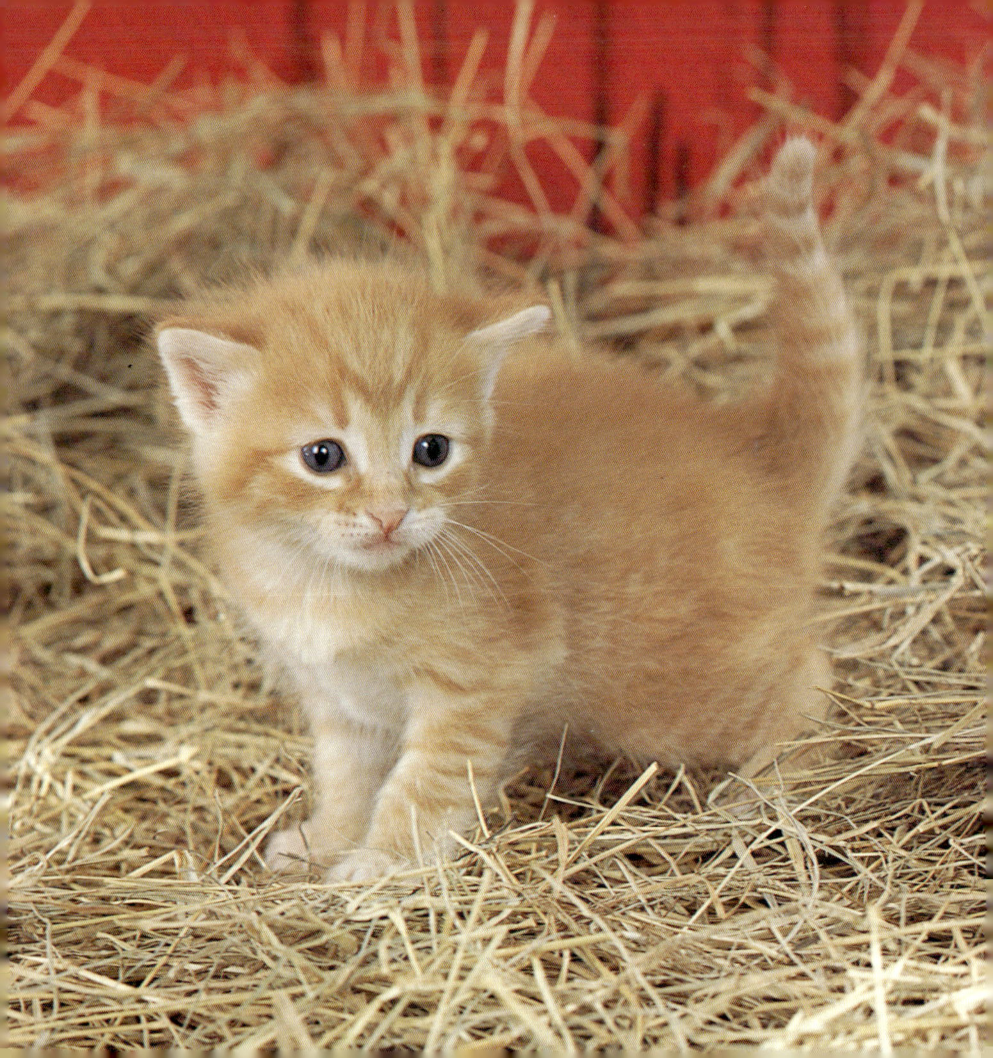

The *smallest* feline is a masterpiece.

—✦—

Leonardo da Vinci

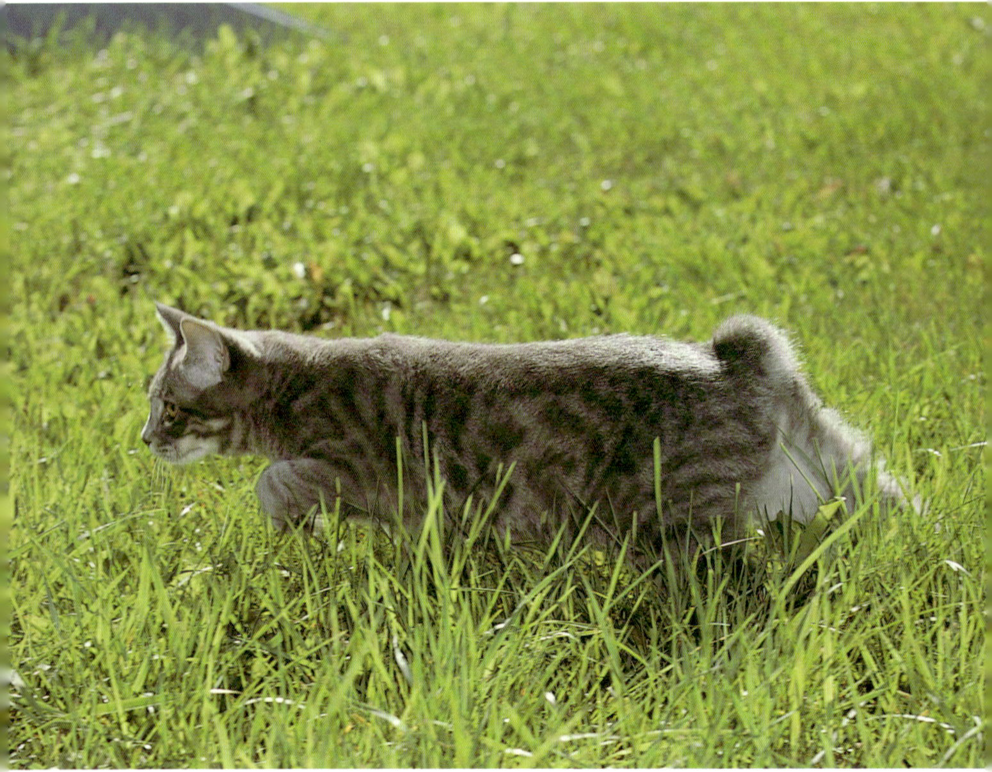

Prowling his own *quiet* backyard or asleep by the fire,

he is still only a whisker away from the *wilds*.

Jean Burden

An *ordinary* kitten will ask more questions

than *any* five year old.

—⊢—

Carl Van Vechten

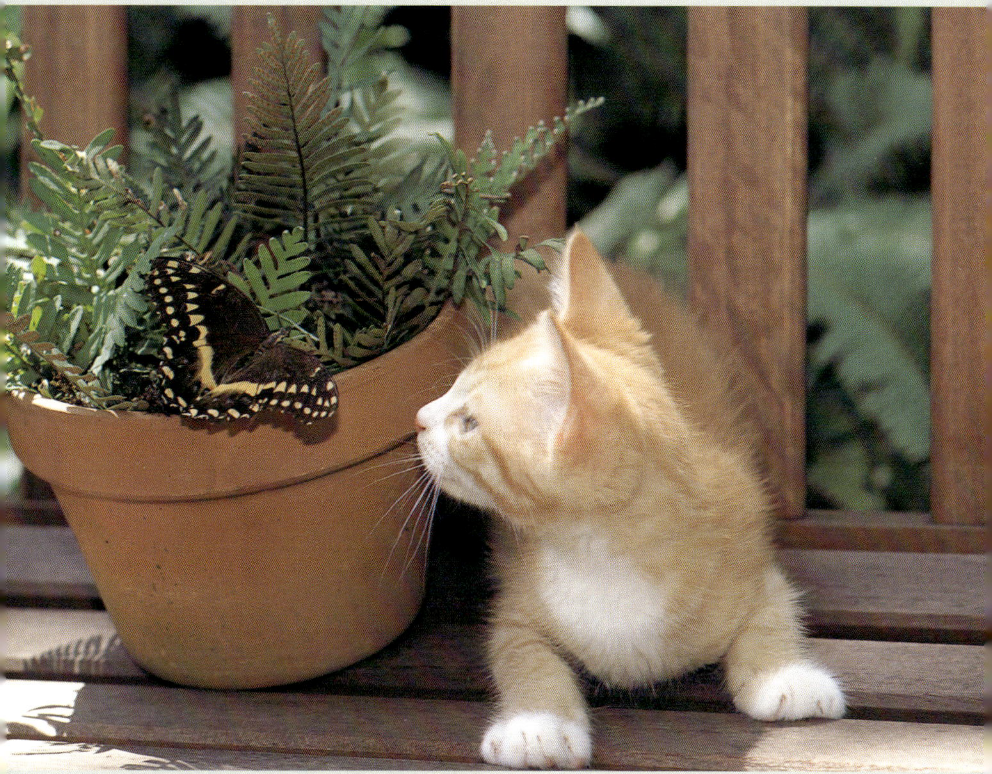

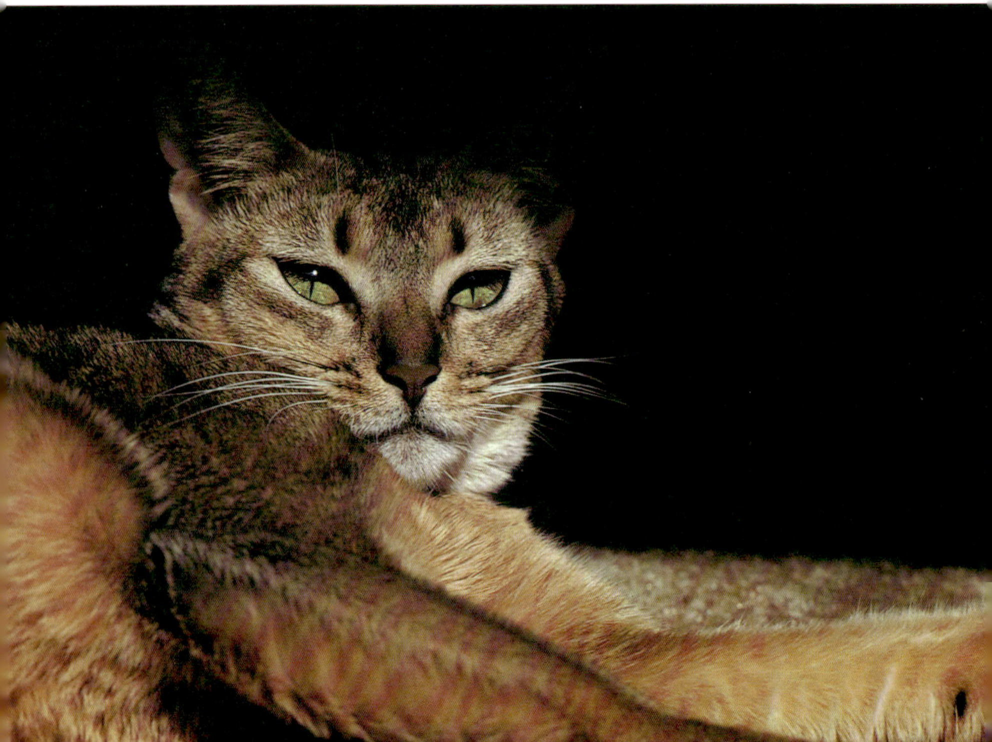

A cat *pours* his body on the floor like *water*.

It is *restful* just to see him.

—•—

William Lyon Phelps

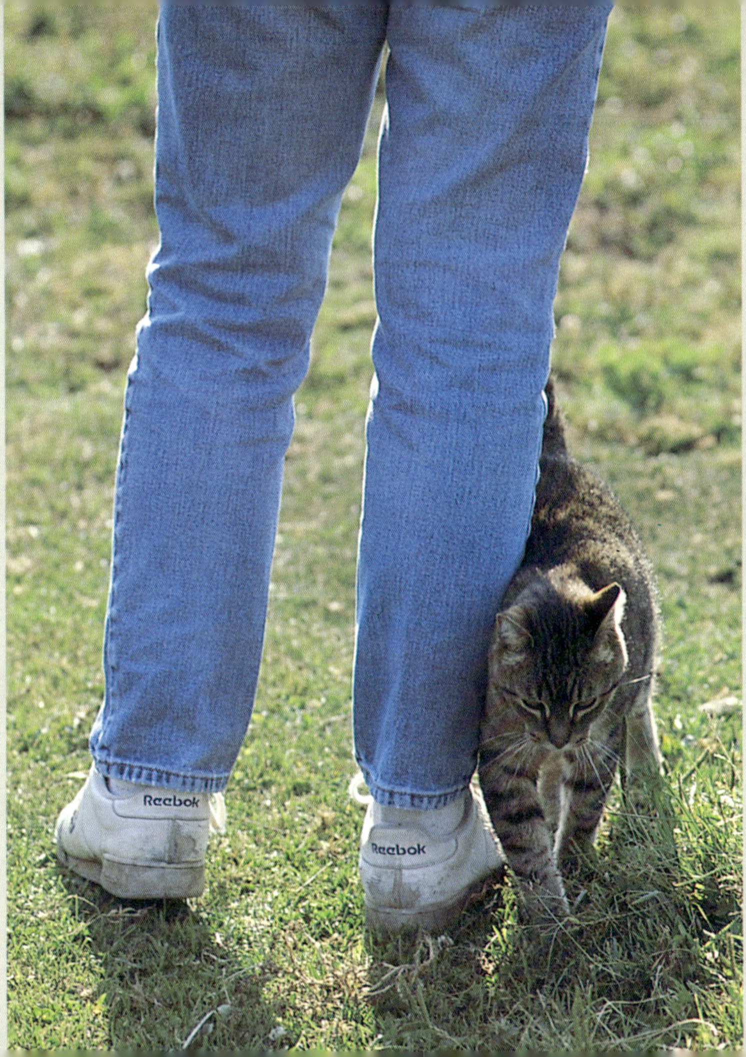
Reebok
Reebok

A cat can *purr* its way out of *anything*.

Donna McCrohan

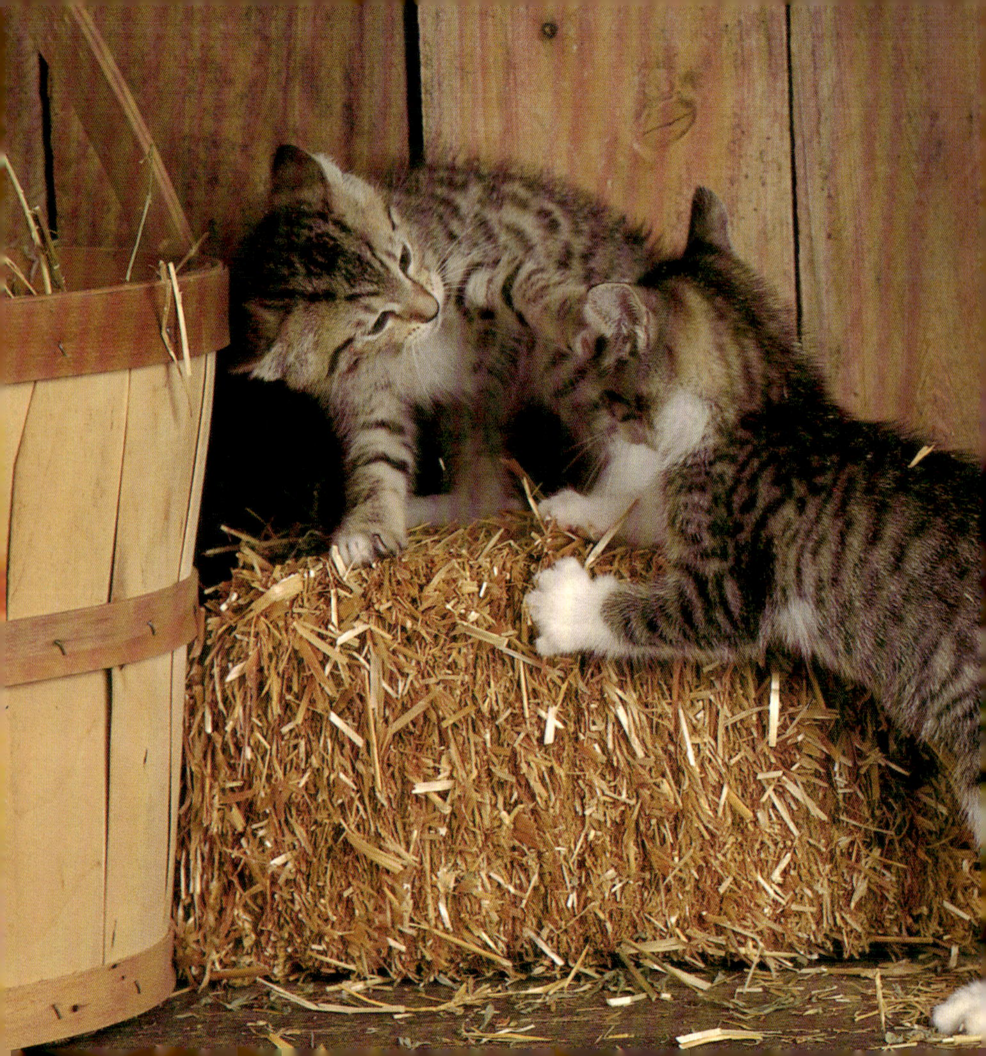

One is *never* sure, watching

two cats washing each other,

whether it's *affection*,

the *taste*, or a trial run

for the *jugular*.

Helen
Thomson

Just as the would-be debutante will *fret* and *fuss* over every detail till all is *perfect*, so will the fastidious feline patiently *toil* until every whisker tip is in place.

Lynn Hollyn

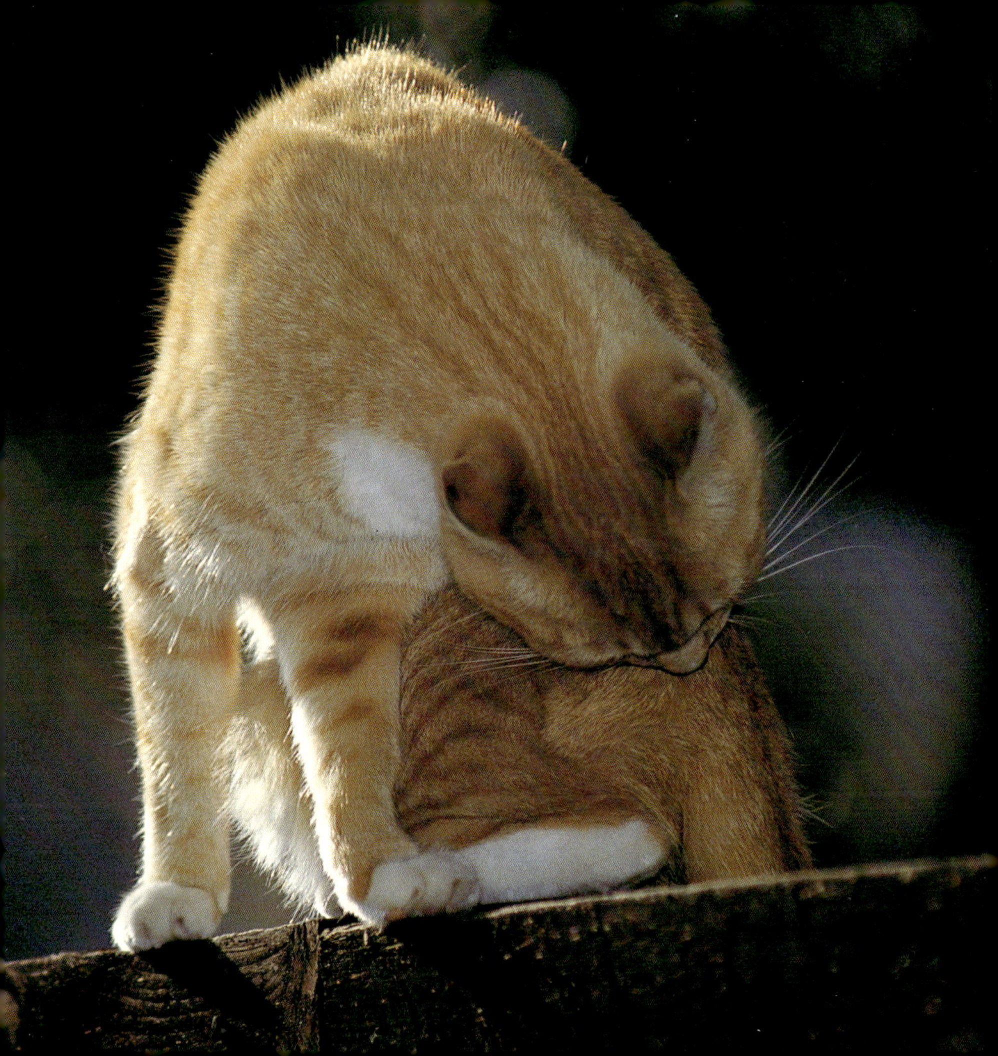

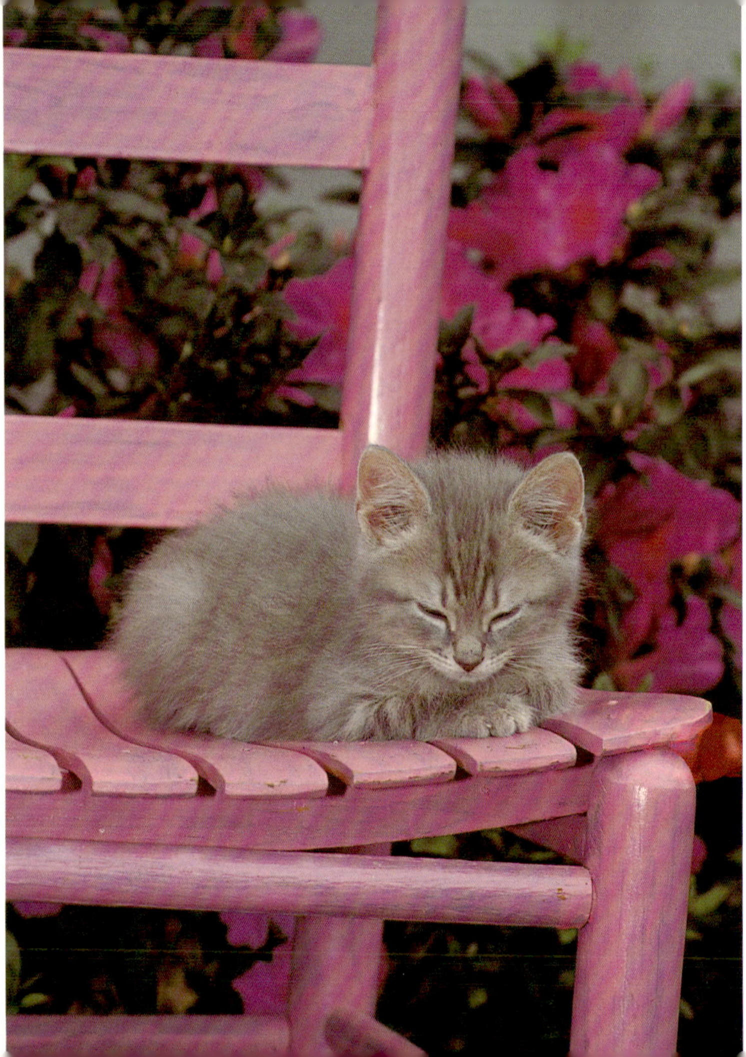

You *cannot* look at a sleeping cat and feel *tense*.

—◆—

Jane Pauley

What *greater* gift than the *love* of a cat?

—⁂—

Charles Dickens

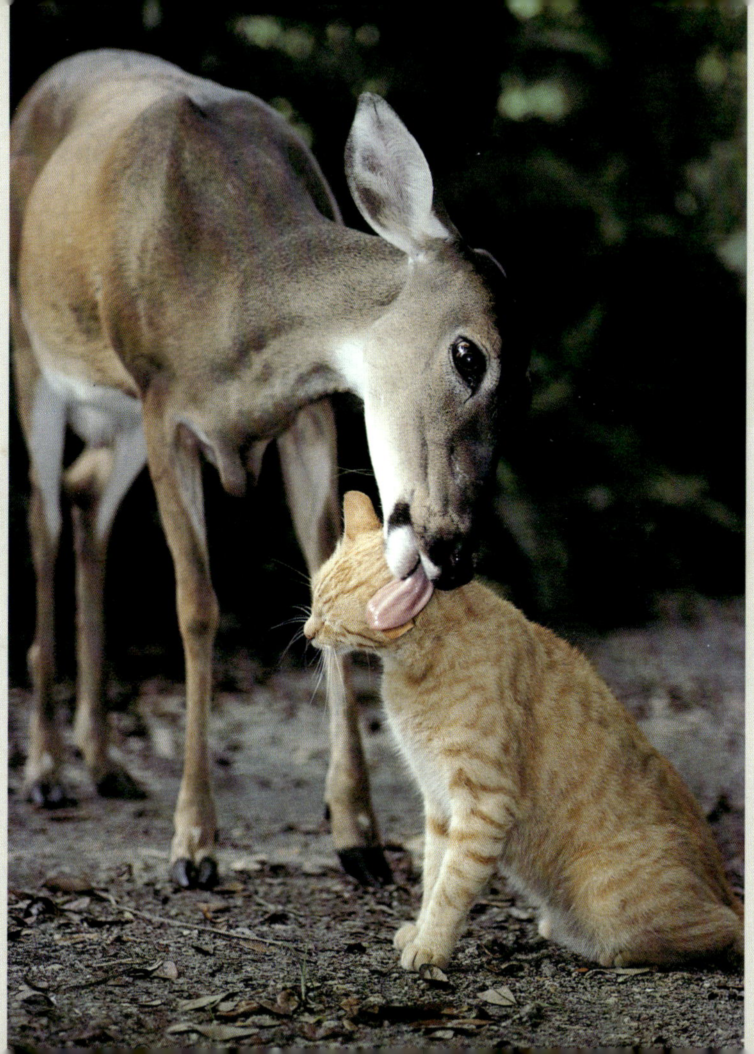

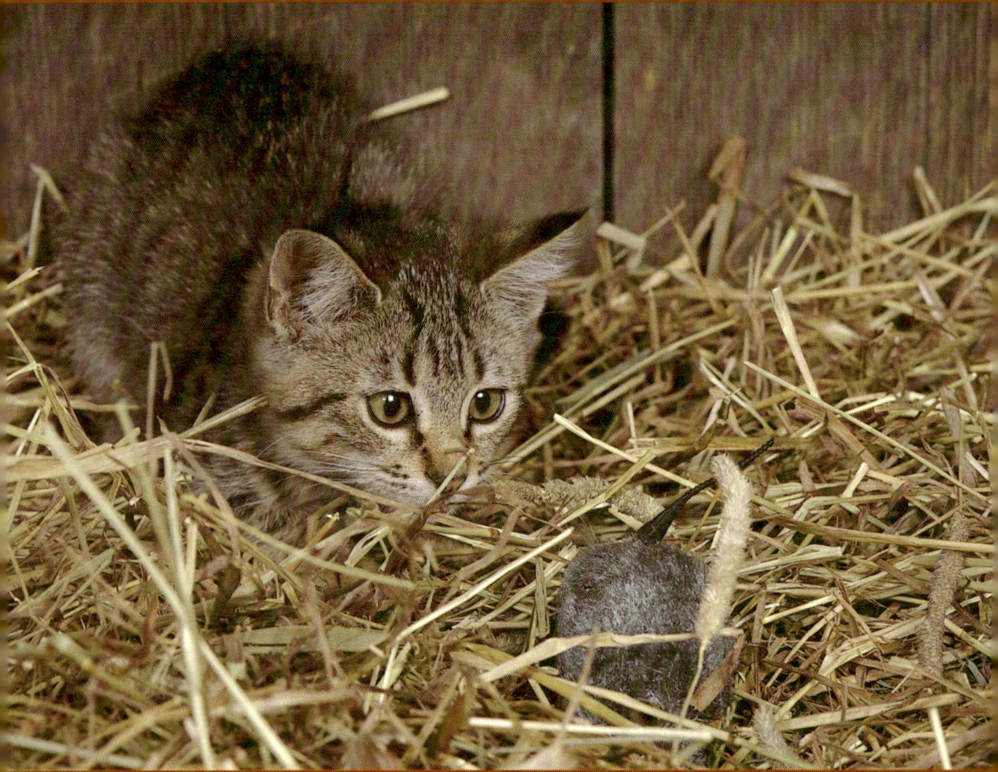

The cat does *not* negotiate with the mouse.

—⊹—

Robert K. Massie

It is in their *eyes* that their *magic* resides.

❖

Arthur Symons

The *cat* has been described as the most *perfect* animal, the acme of muscular *perfection*, and the *supreme* example in the animal kingdom of the *coordination* of mind and muscle.

Roseanne Ambrose Brown